# Three Essential Steps

## Writings by the Author

These and other books available through:
Mystics of the World
Eliot, Maine
www.mysticsoftheworld.com

# Three Essential Steps

## Marie S. Watts

# Three Essential Steps

Mystics of the World First Edition 2015
Published by Mystics of the World
ISBN-13: 978-0692428146
ISBN-10: 0692428143

For information contact:
Mystics of the World
Eliot, Maine
www.mysticsoftheworld.com

Cover graphics by Margra Muirhead
Printed by CreateSpace
Available from Mystics of the World and Amazon.com

৯ ৶

Marie S. Watts

Originally published 1959

# Contents

# To the Reader

This book, *Three Essential Steps*, is one of the most important and powerful messages of the Ultimate. Its importance lies in the fact that it reveals the omnipresence, the universality, and the eternality of all existence. It also reveals the inseparable Oneness that is the Universe, the Identity, and the Body.

This book was first published in 1959, and it was intended only for the members of that class. However, there were so many requests for additional copies that more were printed. It is now being studied in virtually every free nation. The message has been, and continues to be, a tremendous source of inspiration and enlightenment to many sincere students of the Ultimate. Furthermore, it has been the fulfillment of a specific and necessary purpose in the ever continuing revelation of the Ultimate. The absolute truths herein presented are known to be a firm foundation for ever greater Self-revelation.

When *Three Essential Steps* was being written, there was no awareness of the fact that it was to be the foundation for the classes that followed. Now that this fact is apparent, it is clear that some revisions were necessary in order that this book may completely fulfill the purpose for which it was revealed. Therefore, the reader will find some changes in the words and sentences. However, the basic, absolute Truth herein presented cannot be changed: God is All, All is God.

There is a far greater clarification of the truths formerly revealed, and the power of these truths is more apparent.

You, the reader, may question the frequency of our use of capital letters throughout this volume. It may, at first glance, appear that we are inconsistent in our capitalization of certain words. However, upon further study, it will become apparent that any words signifying God are capitalized. This is true because, actually, every noun really is a symbol for the one all-important word, *God*. For instance, the word *Activity* is capitalized whenever it signifies God. God really *is* all activity. But you will note that if this word *activity* refers to assumptive man in action, it is not capitalized. It is our hope that the power of the message will prevail over any agreement or disagreement with the manner in which this message is presented.

Finally, we are firmly convinced that this revised edition will fulfill its purpose in and as the experience of every student who reads and contemplates the absolute truths herein revealed.

Marie S. Watts

# What Is the Universe?

There are three steps to be taken by anyone who is seeking to realize perfection. It makes no difference whether he is seeking to realize this perfection for himself or for someone else. It makes no difference whether the seeming problem may appear to be physical, whether it may appear to be mental, or have something to do with human relationships. There are three steps that *must* be taken. It is our purpose to discover the nature of these three steps, to understand how to take them, and, most important of all, to know why we are taking them—to understand why it is essential to take these three steps,

First of all, let me assure you that you will find no dualism in this work. We stay constantly and without interruption with the fact that God is All. Let me also assure you that every truth that you could ever realize, every truth that anyone could tell you, must have its basis in this one fact: God is All.

There are some, of course, who feel that the Ultimate is too absolute for them. Occasionally someone will say, "I don't feel that I'm quite ready for this. It's too impractical for everyday living." Well, of course, if we have found some message that completely satisfies us, that solves our problems, we are apt to stay with that teaching. That is as it should be. It is perfectly right to stay with any particular teaching so long as that teaching feels right to us, satisfies us, and solves our problems. But there are many of us who find that it is essential to see farther than just the solving of problems. We are not satisfied. We feel that we must expand this Consciousness in greater revelation. We are not satisfied with just "making a demonstration." We are not satisfied with a little better health, a little fuller purse, or a slight betterment in human relationships.

We know that all this is right and normal. We also know that this is only an infinitesimal aspect of this glorious, unlimited Truth. We discover that we are healthier, wealthier; we are more joyous; our relationships are more harmonious. But we realize that the outward manifestations of Truth are not the main issue; they are not satisfying to our constant inner yearning, our constant inner desire to really *know* God, experience God. So we are dedicated in our search for the full and complete revelation of all Truth—the full and complete revelation of the nature of God—thus, the full and complete revelation of all that *we* are.

There are groups meeting all over the world who are just as dedicated as we are. These seekers are not content to merely see a little more gain in health, wealth, or whatever. There is a worldwide spiritual underground. So, you can see, we don't have a monopoly on this search. Who could have a monopoly on Truth? Who could monopolize God?

What individual or group of individuals, what church or organization, what nation or group of nations could monopolize God? "They shall all know me, from the least of them unto the greatest of them" (Jer. 31:34). Why, the Ultimate itself is being studied all over the world, and there are many authors and teachers of this Truth who are being heard, studied, or read throughout the world. You who are reading this work are among this dedicated group, this spiritual underground.

Now let us ask this question: why are we reading this? Are we attempting to discover more truth about God? Are we attempting to discover more truth about the Universe or an Identity outside of or other than ourselves? No! We are never going to discover one single truth about anything or anyone outside our own Identity. We are going to realize why we cannot discover any truth outside ourselves. Actually, our search is for the Truth that *is* our own Being. We really *are* every truth that we could ever discover.

Jesus said, "I am the truth" (John 14:6). He knew what he was talking about. He had to make that discovery just the same as you and I are making it. I am convinced that he had to go along the same path that we are pursuing, dedicating himself (as we are) to the revelation of all truth. Thus, he discovered (as we are discovering) that he (God, identified *as* his Identity) was all the truth that he could know.

This leads us to this fact: all revelation is Self-revelation. You may question, "How can this be?" The answer to this question is contained in one of the most important statements you will ever encounter, namely, "Your Consciousness is your Universe." No matter what is revealed, although it might seem to be revealed to you, it is not revealed *to* you at all. It is revealed *as* you, as your own Consciousness, because it is revealed to be your own Consciousness. It is revealed to be your Universe.

Again, your Consciousness is your Universe. It is revealed to be the truth, the joy, the peace, the glorious perfection that is your Universe. Does it come from the outside? No! No! No truth ever comes to us from outside our own Consciousness. Every truth that seems to be revealed from outside is simply our own God Consciousness, our own God-Being, revealing Itself from within—right where It has always been and will ever continue to be.

This is the reason why I am so insistent that I cannot *teach* you anything. The very most that I can do is to point to the door of your own Consciousness. The reason that you may not have realized this before is that there has seemed to be a little mist (mistaken sense) that hid the glory of your own Being. Once you have begun to even glimpse your Self as you really are, this awareness will continue to expand until you realize that you were never restricted, never confined, neither were you ever limited.

Also, there never was an obstacle to your perception of your Self as you are. You have never been blocked off in space. You have never been hemmed in. You have never been separated from the *One All God Consciousness*. You couldn't have been, because you couldn't have been separated from your Self. Neither could you be separated from your discovery of this glorious Self. So, you see, all revelation is Self-revelation. All discovery is Self-discovery. You don't need to go far to discover your Self, do you? When you discover the limitless, perfect, glorious Self, you may rest assured that you have discovered God. Why? Because God *is* your Self.

You may feel that you are searching for God as though It were some power or presence outside your own Being. But when you really discover God, you experience God right within your own Self—you experience God being your own Consciousness. Does this mean that God is limited? No! God is infinite, unrestricted, unlimited; but God is right here as your own Consciousness, just the same. Furthermore, God is just as much God, equally God, right here *as* you as He is God throughout the Universe. God *is* the Universe, so God is equally expressed throughout Itself as all that exists of the Universe. There is no more of God as one than as another. There is no more of God identified as one than as another. Again, all revelation is Self-revelation. When we have discovered the Self, we have discovered God.

The more we are aware of our genuine and *only* Self the more we are aware that God *is* that Self. (Of course, we are not talking about a little misidentification called a person.) But in the discovery that God is the only Self, we also realize that God is all that exists as the Identity of anyone or anything. No matter what nametag you may have attached to the little false sense of self, each Identity has but one name—I AM. "I am the Lord, and there is none else" (Isa. 45:5).

At the start of this session, we spoke of the three essential steps in the realization of Perfection. The first step in this realization is the revelation of the nature of the Universe Itself, the perfect nature of the perfect Universe.

The nature of the perfect Universe is not the nature of an ebbing and flowing perfection. It is not a perfection that is here today and gone tomorrow. It is not a perfection that is present this week and absent next week or next year. Rather it is a Perfection that is constant, without interruption, a Perfection that constantly reveals Itself to be more glorious and beautiful all the while.

Again, the first step in the realization of this eternal, uninterrupted Perfection is the revelation of the perfect nature of God *as* the Universe. What comprises the Substance, the Forms, the Activity, the Government that constitute this perfect Universe?

The second step in this discovery is the revelation of the individual Identity. What is the individual

Identity? What is Its substance? What is Its activity? What governs It? Above all, *why is* It? Why are you? Why am I? Why is each one of us an individual Identity? Why does each one of us exist as a *specific* Identity? Why am I? What is my purpose? What is my function? Or, to put it more accurately, what is God's purpose in being the specific *I* that I am? Ah, there is the important question—one that each one of us should contemplate again and again every day.

Now, there are some who write and teach in the Absolute who say that there is no such thing as an individual Identity. Of course, we know that our friends who follow Hinduism hope that through progressive reincarnation they will merge into the Infinite All and finally attain what they call Nirvana, where there is no *specific* Identity.

Somehow, I just cannot accept this theory. I am sure that each individual exists, and exists eternally, as that specific Identity. But again, the most important question is: why am I a specific Identity? The answer to this important question will be presented in the next session.

Let us now state briefly the three essential steps in the discovery of the perfect, eternal Self.

What is the Universe?
What is the Identity?
What is the Body?

Our subject for this session is:
What is the Universe?

Before we go into an exploration of this subject, I should like to answer a silent question that is being asked right now. "Why should I be concerned with the Universe? Why is an understanding of the nature of the Universe necessary to me, when my primary concern is the discovery of *my* spiritual Self-hood?"

Believe me, my friends, you are never going to discover your genuine and *only* Self—you are never going to know the genuine and *only* nature of this Self—until you perceive the genuine and *only* nature of the Universe. Why? Because God comprises the Universe. God comprises *you*. It is the same God identified *as* you, as your entire Life, Mind, Being, and Body, that is identified as the Infinite All which is the Universe. You will remember this quotation: "The heavens declare the glory of God" (Ps. 19:1). This is the truth. The very heavens consist of God identifying Itself. When you know, really *know*, the nature of the Substance, Form, and Activity that comprise the Universe, you will really know the nature of the Substance, Form, and Activity that comprise all there is of you.

Now let us return to our subject for this session: what is the Universe? Someone will say, "Why, that is easy; God is the Universe." This is so; there could be no greater truth than this. God is the Universe. But it isn't enough to just make this statement. I know; I have said it, and it wasn't enough. I have heard others say it, and it wasn't enough. Why wasn't it enough? Because we were speaking "words without knowledge."

It isn't enough to say that God is the Universe unless you *know* what God *is* as the Universe. It isn't enough to just say, "God is the Universe," unless you know the nature of God, unless you know the Substance that is God, unless you know the Activity that is God—unless you know what God is as the Substance, Form, and Activity that are all that comprise this Universe.

To make these statements without really knowing their spiritual significance is very much the same as saying, "God is All; God is my Supply; God is my Substance and my Life," and then, "How am I going to pay the rent next month?" or, "Well, I guess I'll have to take an aspirin for this headache." It really is pointless to make these statements of Truth unless we go all the way and perceive the spiritual significance of the power in the Truth we are stating.

So, you see, it isn't enough to just say, "God is the Universe." When we make that statement without spiritual knowledge, we are still not enlightened; we are not illumined.

What is illumination? This is a much misunderstood word. Frequently this word is spoken of as though to be "illumined" were quite a mysterious, unnatural experience. Nothing could be farther from the truth. There is nothing mysterious about illumination. Let us take the mystery out of these perfectly normal, natural experiences. Actually, illumination is simply your own consciousness when it is enlightened. It is your own enlightened Being.

In this enlightened Consciousness, you see the Universe, the Identity, all *substance, form,* and *activity* as they really are. It is being awake. It is natural to be awake. In this thoroughly wide-awake experience, the seeming dream is obliterated. The dream stuff, the dream forms, the mirage that appears to be matter, simply are nonexistent. You are aware that right here is this glorious, perfect Substance, Form, and Activity that *do* exist. There is no mystery about that, is there? Enlightened Consciousness is perfectly normal. It is abnormal and unnatural to dream that we are all blocked off, restricted, and limited in and as matter. It is abnormal to dream that all Substance, all Form, is constituted of solid matter, blocked off in space. The "mystery" is that we have been so deluded by this nonexistent dream picture that it seemed to be genuine.

When we walk around in enlightened Consciousness, it seems mysterious to us that anyone can be so misled by this blocked-off, so-called material, troublesome universe, this universe with its quarrelsome human minds and imperfect, temporal bodies. Someone has said that Jesus walked around in the dream awake. This is a wonderful way to state what takes place in illumination.

Now let us return to the question, "Why is it important that we know the nature of the Universe?" You might also ask, "How is this going to heal my body or increase my supply? How is it going to bring love, harmony, and completeness into my human relationships and experiences?" Believe me, my friends, when I tell you that *this is the only way.*

I know very well, as do you, that you can get help for your pains or an increase for your purse; you can get love and friendship, to a certain extent; you can get all this, to a certain extent, by the road of affirmations and denials. We have all seen this. Some of us have experienced it. There are those who can realize some limited sense of good by visualizing that which they wish to have materialized. Well, I have been told that that works too, *to a certain, limited extent.*

But is this enough? Has it proved itself to be permanent? Has it always brought about that which was good and right? Hasn't it sometimes developed that the visualization has brought experiences that were not right and good? Isn't it true that the pain can seem to return? Isn't it true that the difficulty may reappear in another form or aspect of the body? If we have demonstrated over it, we have *not* eliminated it from our consciousness.

When we say, "I want a thousand dollars," we have limited ourselves to just one thousand dollars. Why should we limit ourselves to just a thousand dollars? Why one dollar, or five dollars? Let us see through these limitations. Isn't it possible that the consciousness of the manifest supply can be *as great as the Principle* which *is* Supply? We say, "God is our supply." Then let us not limit God *as* our supply.

What about demonstrating or visualizing love, friendship, companionship? Is it satisfying? Is it permanent? Isn't it true that demonstrated love, friendship, companionship can turn sour? All of us have seen it. We have seen this happen. We have seen demonstrated love, visualized companionship turn sour. We have seen it go wrong. So often it is proved to be a mistake. Generally it is temporary, and so often it is proved to be unsatisfactory. Indeed, demonstrations are made sometimes, but it is not only possible, it is probable that the demonstration will not be lasting and it won't be satisfying.

We certainly do not criticize those who are teaching or following one of these paths. If we did, we certainly would have to criticize ourselves, because most of us have come up through one or the other of these paths. We have certainly realized some good, some help, through them too. But there does come that inner insistence to see farther. We can always tell when this is taking place. It is when the words we read are just words—words without inspiration. Furthermore, despite all our "mental work," all our "visualizing," the so-called demonstrations are not forthcoming. This is our signal from within our own God Consciousness that we must expand in our awareness of our genuine and *only* Identity.

We are certainly grateful for each and every step along this way and for those who presented these steps. However, if the unlimited good had been realized from the standpoint of the limitless nature of the Universe, including the Identity, there would have been no further search. If each and every so-called healing had been permanent; if the increase in supply had been sufficient; if the love had been satisfying, complete, fulfilling, we would have ended the search right there. But we didn't end it there because it wasn't enough.

Why have we continued on and on in our search? Because we had to continue. We didn't have any choice. "Ye have not chosen me, but I have chosen you" (John 15:16). God is ever revealing Itself as all there is of each and every one of us.

It may have seemed that we were searching. It may even appear that we are searching now. I have had this experience of falsely believing that I was searching. I even became a little impatient and self-righteous about it. All of this is over when we know that we are never going to find God *outside* our own Consciousness. It has always been God Consciousness, identified as the Consciousness of each and every one of us, saying:

> "I am right here, revealing My Self, and you can't help knowing the *I* that *I* am because you can't help knowing your Self. *I* am that Self, and there is no other."

So, you see, it is God insisting upon revealing Itself, evidencing and manifesting Itself *as* our Consciousness. Once we begin to realize the infinite nature of this Truth, we know that we never had any choice in the matter at all. It insists upon revealing Itself as ever-expanding Consciousness. And we discover that we are not even responsible for this expansion or revelation. We couldn't stop it if we tried. Neither have we any power to bring it about.

There is a point that must be made right here. In the old way of dualism, we were attempting to solve our problems from the level of the problem. Even though we had some results, still we were attempting to hold ourselves right at that level of limitation—the limitation of the problem itself.

It is impossible to continue on in this way because God is always insisting upon identifying His glorious, unlimited nature *as* the entire Life, Mind, Being, and Body of each Identity. We are not allowed to continue on in this limited way indefinitely.

*God is omnipotent.* We who are expanding in the Ultimate are expanding beyond and above that limited problem level. In fact, we are beginning to see that there can be no problem and that there is no level from which a problem can be solved because there is no problem. You can't solve a problem when no problem exists.

This brings us right back to the limitless nature of God, identified as the Universe. Let us ponder that quotation from the Bible, "Do not I fill heaven and earth? saith the Lord" (Jer. 23:24). How many times have we read it? How many times have we said it? *But did we really know the tremendous truth that was being stated right in that quotation?*

Indeed, God does fill heaven and earth. God *is* the heaven and the earth. God is the *only* Substance; God *is* the Substance that is the Universe. God is the very nature of the Universe. That which we call the laws of nature can be so cruel, even brutal. But God is the only nature of the Universe, and God is Love. God, as the nature of the Universe, is not cruel and brutal. It is the nature of Love to be ever kind, gentle, and loving. God is the Mind, the Intelligence—God is the Principle governing Itself as the entire Substance, Life, Activity which is the Universe.

We have read much about the fact that God is Principle. What is the point in God being Principle? Are there innumerable substances and forms being governed *by* Principle? Or is God, Principle, the very Substance, Form, and Activity of that which It governs? *This is one of the most important questions that can be asked.* The Substance, the Form, the Activity *is* God, Principle Itself, in perfect, continuous, Self-government. God, Principle, governs Itself as the very Substance, the Activity, and as the functioning that is the orderly, perfect Activity of the Universe.

God is the Power that holds Itself in complete, uninterrupted perfection as the Universe. God is the Power that maintains, sustains, supports, and governs Itself as the entirety that is the Universe. God is the Power that is continuously Self-sustaining, Self-maintaining, as every star, every planet, every galaxy. God is the Power that is Self-acting, Self-controlled, in rightness and changeless perfection. Now we are beginning to get a little better concept as to what God *is* as the Universe.

The statement that I am going to give you now is of the utmost importance. It can, and may, bring forth your realization of your complete freedom, so it would be well for you to dwell in contemplation on this statement:

> Every Truth that is true of the Universe is a universal Truth. Every Truth that is true *as* the Universe is true as your Universe. Every Truth that is true as the Universe, as your Universe, is true as your entire Life, Being, experience, affairs, and as all that exists as your Body. Your Consciousness *is* your Universe.

Oh, my friends, hold this in your Consciousness. Wonderful revelations take place through the contemplation of this Truth.

Now, I would like to share this with you. Just recently, I have realized that I have *experienced* more revelation of Truth through the contemplation of the heavens than I have realized through the reading of literally hundreds of books on the various religions, the metaphysical and mystical writings. In the quiet contemplation of the illimitable heavens (particularly at night), I have discovered more of what God is *as* the Universe. By the contemplation of the heavens, I have discovered the illimitable, impersonal, glorious, free *rightness* that comprises the Universe.

Above all, I have discovered the glory of perfect beauty — the beauty of infinite, eternal Perfection. In the calm, clear atmosphere of the desert nights, I have experienced a complete opening of Consciousness. All false sense of matter has completely vanished, and I have beheld the Universe that is entirely Spirit, God, maintaining Itself in perfect order and glorious beauty.

Furthermore, I have known that the heavens and "I" were composed of the very same Essence, the same Substance, the same Activity, and it was all God, Good.

Now, I realize that my reading helped to prepare me for this revelation, but it was only the preparation. The revelation had to come from within my own Consciousness. This, my loved ones, is where your revelation takes place — within your own Consciousness, for that is where all Truth is eternally.

Why should this contemplation of the heavens reveal so much more of Truth than I had ever found in books, even including the Bible? Everything that is good, real, true, and genuine is evidenced right here in the heavens, *as* the heavens. All harmony, eternality — the infinite, changeless Perfection which is God — are manifested right here in the skies. You will remember the quotation "The heavens declare the glory of God" (Ps. 19:1). The heavens declare, manifest, evidence His glory. Indeed they do! The Universe is God, glorifying Itself. The stars, the planets, the galaxies, unlimited by time or space, unrestricted by personalities, are evidence that God *is*. These very heavens are God, declaring Its own glorious Being to be *all Existence*.

I never give advice; that is a luxury I do not indulge. But if I could advise anyone, I would say something like this: if the limited world of appearance seems to be oppressive, if you seem limited, restricted, discouraged, or depressed, discover your particular sanctuary. Discover your particular secret place.

You may not need to go to the desert, the ocean, or the mountains. This is just my particular way. After all, you will discover your secret place to be within your own Consciousness. But if you can, and would like the inspiration of the uncluttered, impersonal, quiet skies, by all means go to the desert, the ocean, the mountains; go to that environment that is most inspiring to you.

In the quiet peace of the night, focus your attention on the calm, beautiful sky. Let the silence penetrate, permeate, until it reigns supreme. Literally lose yourself (this little spurious sense of self) in the greatness, the grandeur, of the limitless infinitude of the heavens. Presently you will realize that you are conscious of experiencing a calm, beautiful joy.

You never know silence until it is a joyous silence. This I have discovered. Formerly, I believed that I knew silence when I was just quiet, meditating, or concentrating. But I discovered that the very effort to concentrate, the activity of meditation, interfered with the realization of complete silence. Silence, complete silence, is realized when the Consciousness is full open; thus, there is no thinking or meditating going on at all.

This does not mean that the silence is inactive—quite the contrary. What it does mean is this: the little so-called thinking mind is not trying to be active, to think, or meditate. The activity is all going on *without effort*, within your own Consciousness. You are never as alert, as wide awake, as you are during this joyous silence. You feel it all through you. You experience it. In fact, you experience *being* it.

In this way, you have discovered the true meaning of "the peace of God, which passeth all understanding" (Phil. 4:7). It is a peace that has nothing to do with thinking or meditating. Don't try to mentally reach out to the heavens. It won't work. Just let go. Completely open your Consciousness. Have a feeling of being completely open. (I always find that the palms of my hands are upturned to the heavens. I don't do it deliberately. I am not even aware of it at first. But somehow I must feel more completely open with the palms open to the Infinite.)

Presently all sense of weight, of solidity, is obliterated. There is that glorious awareness that I am comprised of the very same Essence that is the *Universe Itself*. One never tries to propel himself into the heavens. You just feel that the heavens are you, and you are the heavens. All that false sense of a little person, a little "I," just melts away; all the feeling of being bound, restricted, blocked off, disappears. All limitations evaporate in this glorious experience. You no longer feel that you are a temporary mortal with a limited life expectancy. You are fully aware that you are eternal, unlimited by time or space. In other words, you are aware of your eternal, unrestricted, unlimited God-Identity.

It is in this awareness that the hidden splendor that you are is revealed. What has hidden this glorious splendor? The little, egotistical, proud "nothing" that tries to call itself a person — that tries to do something of itself, be something of itself, to possess or to have something of itself. That is what seems to have hidden the splendor that you are.

*But God cannot be hidden.* The splendor, the glorious, free You that you are will reveal Itself in ever-expanding joyous experience. You are the Substance that is the Universe. You are the Mind, the Intelligence, that is intelligently functioning as the activity of this Universe. Oh, my friends, you are going to discover that you are more than one with the Universe, the stars, the planets, the galaxies. *You really* are *just what God is, and God is the Universe.*

Often we hear someone say, "Well, I know that I am one with God. I live by God's grace." So long as we speak in that way, we haven't quite seen it. The use of that little word *with* shows that there is still some misconception that there are two—God *and* you. So long as we say that we live by God's grace, we are making the mistake of believing that God *permits* us to live. It is as though God were one and we were another, depending upon His grace for Life Itself. This is dualism. *We live because God lives as us.* We can't help living. Neither can God help being the Life that he is as our Life. There are not two lives. There is but one Life, and this is the Life that is God, living Its own Life by evidencing Itself *as* our specific Life.

There is no such thing as God *and* you. There is just God *being* you. There is just God *being Itself as you.* There is no use saying that God is All and then saying we are one with God or that we live by God's grace. Either you have no existence at all—you are not conscious, not alive—or God, the one and only Life is living Its own Life as your Life. It is all God being God—God being God *as* you; God being God *as* me; God being God *as* each star and planet, each galaxy. Yes, it is God being God as everything that constitutes the Universe, for God really *is* the Universe. The unlimited, unrestricted God that constitutes the Universe constitutes all there is of you. Thus, these restrictions and limitations are seen to be entirely fallacious and powerless. The peace of this revelation is indescribable.

Does this mean that you lose your Identity? Does it mean that you are not aware that you are a specific Identity? Indeed it does not. Quite the contrary. You are intensely aware of being a specific Identity. But most important of all, you are aware that your Identity is eternal — an eternal Identity. You realize that you never began to be the Identity that you are and you can never stop being the Identity you are. Neither is any human mother or father responsible for the fact that you are the Identity you are. You can't help being the Identity you are because you are God eternally identified as your Identity. You are not even responsible for your Self. God is responsible for being Itself *as* you.

God is responsible for being Its Perfection as your Perfection. God is responsible for being Its Life, identified as your Life. It is necessary that you be alive. It is essential that you live. God would not be living His own Life completely and fully if you were not alive. Your Life is essential to the entirety, the completeness, that is God, Life. (Of course, we know that God has no gender. The words *He* or *His* are simply used because they are generally used to designate God. But God is God, neither masculine nor feminine.)

How could you be any other Identity than the specific Identity that you are? Who could you be unless you were you? Who could you be unless you were God identified as the specific Identity that you are? You are aware that you are you and no one else. Thus, you are aware of being your own specific Identity. This awareness is actually God, aware of being you. God is eternally conscious of being the Identity that you are. So you are eternally conscious of being the Identity that you are—a specific Identity without beginning, change, or ending.

It is of the utmost importance to realize that the Infinity that is God is the Infinity that constitutes the Universe. It is essential to perceive God to be the boundless, immeasurable, unrestricted, timeless, unlimited, spaceless All that is the Universe. It is in this revelation that we realize our own freedom from limitations and restrictions. This perception includes the eternality as well as the immutable nature of the Universe. We perceive God to be Its eternal, beginningless, changeless, endless entirety as the entirety that is this Universe; and here is no solidity, no material measurement.

This Universe is calm, peaceful, orderly, balanced, joyous, and free. This Universe is the "kingdom of heaven." All that is true as this Universe is true as you. You are in the kingdom of heaven right now, and the kingdom of heaven is in you. Of course it is. You are your own heaven.

We are always hearing about "the end of the world." But we never hear anything about the end of the Universe. There will never be an ending for this planet or for the Universe. This planet is included in the Allness that is the Universe. The Universe is God, without beginning, change, or ending.

This planet is essential to the completeness that is God as the Universe. Even some of the physicists are now beginning to say that the Universe may never end, thus It could never have had a beginning. In our enlightened Consciousness, we have already perceived this to be true. But our enlightened Consciousness perceives more than this—we are aware that the Universe is eternally perfect. It is in this awareness that we are aware of our own changeless, perfect nature. It is in this realization that we find freedom. There are no restrictions, no limitations; there is no bondage. Freedom is our answer. Freedom we realize. It is wonderful to know that we are composed of the very Essence that comprises the Universe.

As we contemplate this glorious Truth, we find that we are increasingly aware of the harmony, peace, and order that is evident in the perfect functioning of the stars and planets. Can you imagine a disagreement, a strain, a quarrel, between the stars? This is ridiculous, of course. But as you perceive yourself to be the same Essence and Activity that comprise the Universe, you can readily see how impossible it is for you to experience pain or struggle. The Mind that is the Universe knows no disturbance. It is not a mind that frets or quarrels. It knows no fear and nothing to fear. It is calm, peaceful, beautiful Being.

Perhaps one of our greatest needs right now is the calm and peace of this realization. Why? Because this dream nightmare calling itself the world seems to be so troubled. It seems so fearful. There seems to be such a struggle for power, for wealth. On every side we have an appearance of mental elbowing, so much quarreling, dishonesty, and injustice. So it is vitally important that we realize our oneness with and *as* this calm, peaceful, joyous Universe. I firmly believe that this is why the truth that God is the Universe is being revealed right now.

Now our consciousness is expanding beyond a little personal sense of self. You see, dear ones, this *has* to take place in and as individual Consciousness. This little, limited, personal sense of self is always selfish. It may *seem* to be unselfish, but really it isn't. It doesn't have the power to be unselfish. It doesn't even know how to be unselfish—in fact, *it doesn't know anything*. In the discovery of the genuine and *only* Self, the little mistaken sense of self is dissolved. In this perception, God, the Infinite All, reveals Itself to be the entire Essence and Activity that is your Universe.

Our Consciousness is expanding beyond the little personal sense of self, beyond the limited worried sense of doing something, having something, being something of itself. We are beginning to realize that we are not even responsible for ourselves as someone separate and apart from the one Infinite All, God, Neither are we responsible for any other Identity. The false sense of responsibility for someone else is always the seeming little self, believing that it can do something, that it has power to change something—that it is responsible for someone and can do something to help God help them. Actually, you are not even responsible for your own Self. God is responsible for Himself as the Universe. God is responsible for Himself as everything that is in the Universe. God is responsible for Himself as you.

The eternal *I* that is identified as your Identity knows no false sense of responsibility. It knows no one in need of help. How can God know a need for help when He knows His Perfection to be all that has existence? God knows only Its own Completeness, Its own Perfection. God knows Itself to be Its Supply. In fact, God knows nothing of a need. How can God, who is All, know a need or anyone in need? You can only know that which God knows.

With what mind could you really know a need? What is this falsity called a need? Let us go back of it and see what it means. No matter what the seeming need may appear to be, whether a need for supply as money, a need for health, strength, or a need for calm and peace, it signifies only one thing—it is the very presence of the Supply announcing itself. That which seems to be the need is only an indication that God (the Supply) is already present. All that the seeming need does is to focus our attention upon the Supply, which is already right here. So we do not dwell upon the need. Rather we contemplate *all that God is as the Supply*. Presently we discover that there is no need; there is only the Supply.

Have you ever looked up into the night sky and seen ugliness? I haven't. I don't believe that anyone has ever looked into the calm, beautiful, night sky and seen anything but beauty. Even if the clouds are obscuring the stars and all seems dark, you do not see ugliness. If all is dark, you don't see anything.

There is a great spiritual significance in this. If you are not seeing Beauty, you are seeing darkness, and darkness is nothing. Thus, if you don't see Beauty, you are not seeing anything. If you are not being Beauty, you are not being anything. Darkness is nothingness. To seem to be in darkness is to seem to be nothing. To seem to see darkness is to seem to be aware of nothing. When you look into the sky and see that which is there, you see Beauty. *Thus, you are seeing God because God is Beauty.*

Now, we have perceived God as the Universe Itself. To briefly recapitulate: we have perceived God as Infinity, Eternity, Principle, Peace, and Beauty. Does this mean that God is divided into different elements? No! All that God is, is present wherever God is, and that is everywhere. Thus, all that God is, is equally present as Eternity, Infinity, Peace, Beauty, Principle, Perfection, and as All that God is. God is omnipresent as the genuine nature of every synonym that could be used in an effort to explain what God is. Yes, He is omnipresent as infinitely more than all the synonyms could symbolize.

Let us consider God as Love. God *is* Love. We know that Love is not an attribute of God; neither is Love an attribute of you. Sometimes we seem to feel as though we have the power to love or not to love, the power to give or to withhold love. *We do not have that power.* Love is not an attribute of you, and Love is not an attribute of me. You *are* Love. I *am* Love. We have to love because we are just what God is, as us, and God is Love. God is the Love that you are; God is the Love that I am. We have to love. We have no choice but to love; we can only be what God is, identified as each one of us.

In viewing the Universe, let us consider the beautiful harmony that prevails in the heavens. Each star and planet moves in perfect harmony in its relationship to every other star and planet. No star or planet gets too close to another one. No star or planet moves too far away. There is an attraction, and this attraction holds everything in this Universe in its proper relationship to the All. What is this attraction? Love—Love is the attraction. It is Love that holds all in perfect harmony and perfection; it is Love that functions so harmoniously as the activity of the Universe.

Love and Perfection are the same thing. No wonder they say, "There is no fear in love; but perfect love casteth out fear" (John 4:18). Love, in order to be Love, must be perfect. Perfection, in order to be perfect, has to be Love. The attraction is not personal. It is impersonal.

You will remember the Bible quotation, "Love thy neighbor as thy self" (Lev. 19:18). This has been considered a difficult thing to do. But it becomes simple, easy, and natural when we know the true nature of Love. Of course, we can and do love our neighbor as ourself. We know that our neighbor is the very same Love that is identified as our only Self. Your neighbor is the same Love that you are. How, then, can your neighbor help loving you? True, your neighbor is an individual Identity, just as you are an individual Identity, but it is the same Love identified as each one of you. No one planet imposes upon another; no neighbor, friend, or relative imposes upon another.

So often it seems as though we are being imposed upon. In a situation such as this, it is well to realize that Love and Intelligence are inseparable. We are Love; but we are also Mind, Intelligence. This Intelligence knows when there is an effort to impose; It also knows that this is false and wrong. Intelligence never permits another to impose upon It. It is just as false to permit another to impose upon you as it is for you to impose upon another. Why? Because you would be usurping the right and the necessity of another Identity to realize his own strength and completeness. Thus, you would be in the position of contributing to his *seeming* weakness, or of weakening him. Furthermore, you are assuming a responsibility that is not yours.

This does not mean that we are not kind. Love is always kind. Love is compassionate. *The Love that is also Intelligence knows what to do and when to do it.* It also knows what not to do and when not to do it. Always, in a case that seems to be imposition, it is well to realize that no planet seeks to usurp the orbit or the activity of another planet. No star or planet imposes itself upon another. Approaching something like this from the standpoint of the Universe always helps one to be impersonal in realizing the truth of the situation. Can you see how these truths that are universal are in operation in your Universe?

Again, no planet attempts to usurp the orbit or the activity of another planet. But that is not the way it *appears* to be in the so-called human experience. If we were to judge by appearances, it would seem that someone is always trying to push someone else out of the way in order to have his place or position. In the heavens, there is no grasping for place, no greediness for power or money. There is no displacing or pushing around. Neither is there a complaint that one planet has a favored position over another planet. And, above all, no one star or planet is responsible for another star or planet.

Does this seem preposterous to you? Does it seem to be wandering far afield? Dear friends, let me assure you that this universal approach proves itself as does no other approach that I have ever discovered. It works.

Let me tell you how it works and why it works. *Every truth that you can know is a universal truth.* It is not that you are knowing the truth *about* the stars and planets. It is that you are *knowing the Truth.* This universal approach frees you so that this Truth becomes apparent as the Perfection that has always existed. You are conscious of the limitless Power, Order, and Perfection that is continuously functioning in and as the Universe.

And it is a simple matter to realize that it is this same Power, Order, and Perfection that is *all* that is operating in your Universe. Furthermore, when you contemplate the Perfection that comprises the Universe, you are dispelling the false sense of a little personal self that seems to be in trouble. In short, you stop working on the nonexistent problem and begin to realize the Perfection that does exist. This is no unproved theory. I have seen it prove itself to be the Truth that is Power—not once, but again and again.

To continue: The Intelligence that is the Universe, functioning in, through, and as the stars, planets, and galaxies, is the same Intelligence that is operating, functioning right now, here—in, through, and *as* this planet. It is this same Intelligence that is right here, operating in, through, and *as* you and *as* me.

Do you begin to perceive why it is essential to know that God is the Universe? This is not impractical.

It proves itself in practical, everyday living. Remember, God is the only Power. God is the only Presence operating in, through, and *as* your Universe; in, through, and *as* your experience; in, through, and as your very Body. Again, *your consciousness is your Universe.*

Are we speaking of the stars and planets as though they were material? No! We know better than that. We know that they are not matter. God is Spirit, Life, Mind, Consciousness. How could God be All if those stars and planets were matter?

If God is All, then All is God. All—everything— *has* to be just what God *is*, and God is not matter. Those stars and planets are not matter, but they do exist as Substance, Form, and Activity. Every star, every planet is here, but not one of them is here as a body of matter. *There is no matter.* They exist as Form; they are active; they are Substance. But God, Spirit, is all Substance and all Activity. If they exist at all (and they do), they have to exist as just what God is.

There is nothing in existence but God. But remember this: they exist as just what God is, as each specific Form, Substance, and Activity. I am sure that if the physicists could really see the heavenly bodies as they are, they would realize that there are no two of them exactly alike. There are no two of us exactly alike either. Each star and planet is that specific Identity; and each one of us is that specific Identity. Even so, it is the same God, the same Principle, Life, Truth, Love, Mind, Soul that is identified as each and every specific Identity.

Those stars and planets that seem to be matter are but the dream's distorted pictures of the heavenly bodies—a misinterpretation of the spiritual, perfect, harmonious, eternal bodies. The genuine stars and planets are that which the dream is about. But there couldn't be a dream *about* those stars and planets unless they really existed. Actually, the genuine stars and planets are that Reality which the dream is about. But they are not the way the dream pictures them. They do have form; they are Substance in form; but we must never forget for one moment that they are not matter.

Now, let us consider God as Principle. How I used to shy away from that word *Principle*. I could say, "God is Love." I gloried in saying that. But I always shied away from the word *Principle*. It seemed cold, unloving, and distant. Then one day I realized that there is order, dominion, and power in operation in the Universe.

I also perceived that everything functioned in complete harmony. And I knew that where there is such harmony, there must be Love. I could see that there could not be such dominion, power, and perfect order functioning in the Universe unless it were Principle in active government. But when I observed how harmoniously each star and planet functions in its relationship to the other heavenly bodies, I realized that this dominion, power, and order must be Love.

Suddenly one day I burst forth with these words: "But it's a *loving* Principle." Then I could see that you cannot separate Principle from Love because God is complete. Wherever He is, whatever He is, God is complete *as that*. Then I knew that Principle and Love are one, and that One is God, Love — eternal and infinite.

There is another aspect of that word *impersonal* that I would like to mention. So often when we speak of Love as impersonal, we seem to arouse a sense of antagonism. This is because so often impersonal Love is mistakenly considered to be cold, unsympathetic, and without compassion. Nothing could be further from the truth. I can assure you that impersonal Love is anything but cold. Impersonal Love is the greatest, the most compassionate, the most unselfed, giving Love in existence.

Actually, we don't know what Love is until we know what it is to love impersonally. When we know impersonal Love, we really experience Love. We Love because we can't help loving. We have no choice. We love because we *are* Love. And believe me when I tell you that it is not cold. It is warm and beautiful. We know what impersonal Love is by being Love Itself. We have neither the power to give nor to withhold Love. We cannot help being just what God is as our Identity. God is Love, and God is

Love as every Identity. When we know this truth, we really love.

Let us observe the impersonal, loving Principle functioning as the Activity of the Universe, the planets, the galaxies. Here all is sustained, all is maintained constantly—and when I say "constantly," I mean without interruption. All is maintained constantly in perfect order. There is never a mistake. There is never anything haphazard about the divine order of the heavens. Love holds all in perfect order, functioning perfectly in order that the whole, the entire Universe, may be maintained and sustained in perfect harmony and perfection. This is the Principle that is Love in constant operation.

There is never a mistake in the orderly functioning of the Universe. There is never an interruption in this orderly functioning. In Principle, two and two are not five. In Principle there can be no mistakes. In Principle there can be nothing that can be, or can become out of order. In Principle there is never anything haphazard. In Principle there is nothing out of its orbit, out of place. In Principle the Identity is always conscious of Its eternal, unin-terrupted nature. In Principle the body is always consciously perfect.

If there could be imperfection, there would be no Principle. If there could be imperfection, God would not be All. If there could be imperfection, then you would have to have Principle including errors—intelligent Principle making mistakes. This is impossible.

We hear a lot about the end of the world. Let us examine this belief that the world must come to an end. Why is this fallacy accepted by almost everyone? It is because everything that seems to be confined to a limited sense of existence is supposed to be limited. The more confined it seems to be, the greater the limitation seems to be.

For instance, we can compare a pinpoint in infinity to a split second in eternity. Incidentally, some day it will be known that that which is called time and that which is called space are one and the same thing. Actually, there is no such thing as time and space. There are two words that reveal the spiritual significance back of these words *time* and *space*. These two words are *here* and *now*. There is no "here and there." There is only *here*. There is no "now and then." There is only *now*.

However, if we were to consider the Earth from the standpoint of space, this planet would be but a pinpoint in infinity. And if it were composed of matter, its existence would be but a split second in eternity.

But we must remember that to those on Mars or some other planet this planet is as eternal and as changeless as is the Universe. Our belief that the world must come to an end stems from the dream that we are limited, restricted, confined to this one little planet. Everything that is misinterpreted to be matter is believed to be temporary, to have beginning, change, and ending. The Universe is considered to be limitless in space, so we do not regard it as limited in time. The Earth planet seems to be limited in space, so it is considered to be limited in time.

Another reason we hear so much about the end of the world is that our planet seems so close to us. It is as though we were restricted and confined to this planet. But are we? Indeed we are not. I can assure you that we are not confined to this so-called Earth planet. Many of you who are reading this right now *know* that you are not confined to this planet. You who have experienced illumination (enlightened Consciousness) have perceived the unrestricted, limitless nature of your Being, and you *know* that you are not confined to this or any other planet.

When we see that we are unconfined, when we see that this planet is as indestructible and imperishable as is every other planet in this Universe, we will stop talking of the end of the world. The world can no more come to an end than can the Universe. Why? Because this planet is a specific Identity in the eternal Allness that comprises the Universe. This planet is essential to the completeness that is this Allness. No one expects Mars, Jupiter, Venus, or any other of the planets to come to an end. We don't limit them by timing their existence. Indeed, there is not one single star or planet in the Universe that is limited in its existence. God is the Universe, and God is eternal, infinite. God is the Universe, and

God is eternally and infinitely complete. That is why the world, including you and me, cannot come to an end. That is why the Universe, with all its stars, planets, and galaxies, cannot come to an end.

Every truth that is true of the Universe is true of you. Every truth that is true of a planet is true of you. Why? Because every truth that is true is true *as you*. Remember the statement of Jesus: "I am the truth." He knew what he was talking about.

Now we have arrived at some very important questions. Does this planet exist of itself? Does any star or planet exist of itself? Is any star or planet responsible (of itself) for its own existence? Can any star or planet act of its own volition? Can it refuse to act? Can it slow itself? Can it move itself out of position, out of its own orbit? Can any star or planet do anything of itself? Can any star or planet be anything of itself? Can it govern or control itself, separate itself, become separate from the one all-omnipotent All? The answers to all these questions will reveal themselves to be in the negative. The important point for you to remember is that every truth that is true of the stars and planets *is true of you*.

The entire Substance, Form and Activity of each and every star and planet is the one all-omnipotent Principle. This Principle is also Mind, Consciousness, Life, Love, Perfection, Beauty performing Its function, fulfilling Its purpose by being that specific star and that specific planet. The entire government, the entire activity that is functioning right now, is the all-omnipotent Presence revealed *as* that specific star or that specific planet.

So you see, dear friends, that while there are infinite, innumerable stars and planets, they are all one Essence, one Substance, and one Activity. Each one is a specific Identity, yet it is *the same omnipotent Perfection identified as each Identity*. Their Activity is the same omnipotent Intelligence in harmonious action. So they are all One; each one individual, each one a specific Identity, *but all are One.*

Does Mind govern these heavenly bodies as though they were matter, as though they were solid masses? Does Mind govern these bodies as though they were something different or other than Itself? No indeed; that could not be. In order to govern the stars and planets, Mind *has* to be the very Substance, the very Essence that constitutes their Substance, their Essence.

Now, it is clear that the entire Universe, including each and every Identity, is the one God, Mind, Consciousness, Life identifying and revealing Itself. Whatever has Form is God-substance in Form. Whatever has Activity is God being active. What ever has Life is God living as that Life. Whatever has Form, Life, Activity, is beautifully perfect and perfectly beautiful. Infinite Mind is not just something that is up there around those heavenly bodies, making them behave themselves. Mind is each planet and star, governing Itself as that specific

Identity. It is all Mind governing, evidencing Itself to be the very Substance and Activity of all existence. "The earth is the Lord's, and the fullness thereof; the world, and they that dwell therein" (Ps. 24:1). Yes, the Earth is the Lord's; the Universe is the Lord's because the Universe *is* the Lord. The Universe is God. The stars, planets, galaxies, all Existence is God.

How does this concern us? What does this mean in our experience? It means this: the same Power, the same eternal Perfection that comprises the Universe comprises each and every one of us. The revelation of the unlimited nature of the Universe opens our Consciousness to our unlimited spiritual nature. Our attention is drawn away from the little personal misidentity, and thus our glorious, free, joyous, unlimited God-Self becomes apparent as our *only Self.*

Now, in closing this session, there is one thing more that I would like to tell you—namely, that if you will maintain this revelation of the *limitless Rightness that is the Universe,* persistently in and as your Consciousness, you will find that it will expand, even when you are seemingly asleep. You won't need to try to bring this about. This expansion of Consciousness will just obliterate the little personal sense of self because you have *withdrawn your attention* from that *misrepresentation* of what you are. The morning awakening will reveal existence in greater clarity; you will discover that many of the seeming shackles have fallen away. You will also experience a greater sense of peace and a keener perception of the unlimited, free nature of the Universe, the Identity, and the Body.

# What Is the Identity?

Before we explore the main theme of our subject for this session, let us answer some questions that were presented at the end of the last session. These are good questions, and they reveal much spiritual insight on the part of the questioners.

The first question is, "Do you believe in deep meditation? If you do, how long should this meditation continue?"

You will notice that in my writings the word *meditation* is rarely used. This is also true in my classwork and in interviews. While I do occasionally use this word, I really prefer the word *contemplation*. When I became aware of the fact that I was increasingly saying *contemplation* instead of *meditation*, I questioned as to just why this should be true. Turning to *Webster's Dictionary*, I found the following definition: "Meditation: Act of meditating; close or continued thought." And a wonderful definition of the word "contemplation" is: "Act of viewing steadfastly and attentively." In studying the various definitions of these words, I discovered that it is possible to use them interchangeably, but for the most part, there is a definite difference in the semantics of the two words.

For instance, "close or continued thought" involves a *thought process*. This thought process in turn involves *reasoning*. Viewed in this light, the word *meditation* is misleading for that which takes place in the glorious silence of true enlightened perception.

Actually, a process of thought has to do with the so-called human mind. It is not until this misrepresentation of Mind is completely obliterated that God, Mind, Consciousness is realized. The Mind that is God does not think — It *knows*. Thinking implies time, and thought process would require time in which to arrive at some given point or conclusion. The one and only Mind is not a thinking Mind. I rarely use the word *Mind* except in referring to Intelligence.

The act of "viewing steadfastly and attentively" is something else again. This is exactly what takes place in silent contemplation. We do not think our way into this Ultimate silence. Rather, we become *full open* to revelation. This complete opening of Consciousness is only attained through the absolute certainty that of ourselves we are nothing, can do nothing, know nothing, be nothing. When this complete, unselfed awareness is realized, we can then know that we are in silent contemplation. Our entire attention is engaged in viewing steadfastly the glorious, changeless Perfection that already is all Existence. Indeed, I do believe in this kind of contemplation.

I cannot speak of time in connection with this experience. Sometimes it may be what the world would call a matter of moments; yet to me it is eternity itself. Sometimes I remain in this contemplation hour after hour throughout the day and night. Yet to me it is but a second. So, you see, there really is no time element in genuine contemplation. It is possible for one to go about his daily affairs, meeting and talking with others, and yet remain in this illumination. You move about, you listen, you answer, yet none of these things move you. You are untouched by everything that pertains to a so-called human world.

This is not an abnormal experience. On the contrary, *it is the only normal experience.* To those who meet you and talk with you, there is no change. Oh, they generally remark upon how well or how happy you look. But they are only seeing the illusory picture of you, while you are viewing them and everything as it really is rather than the way it appears to be.

Now, you may be questioning something like this: "But what shall I do if I am seeking Light on some particular problem or situation?"

Dear friends, there is only one way to perceive the Light on any specific situation. Eliminate completely the little, self-important "I." *Be full open with no reservations.* Let the Mind that is God reveal Itself to be your only Mind, your only Consciousness. This is truly *being* that Mind that was in Christ Jesus. Everything takes place in and as God. If there is some specific subject upon which you are seeking

Light, it is well to begin to question about that particular subject.

Right now, I must emphasize that it is futile to ask any question unless you listen for the answer. Actually, the listening is more important than the questioning. The questioning only serves to focus your attention upon that particular subject. Always know that the answer to that specific question already exists. If it didn't, it would never occur to you to ask the question. What you really are doing is simply opening your Consciousness completely for the revelation of the already existing answer to that distinct question.

Where does the answer exist? *Right where the question was asked.* The answer exists right here and now in and *as* your Consciousness. Remember, there is one Consciousness—one Consciousness that can be conscious as your Consciousness. You could not be conscious as a Consciousness in which the answer to your question is absent. Sometimes the answer to your specific question will not be revealed immediately. Again, you may have to ask this specific question over and over again. But rest assured of one thing—*the answer will be revealed*.

You will know it to be true with a solid conviction. Just don't try to answer your own questions by thinking, reasoning, or straining for the answers. It won't work. You have opened Consciousness for the answer to that question; listen silently until the answer is clear or until you realize the beautiful peace that assures you that all is well and that you need have no doubts or reservations about the answer. Having done this and experienced this, just leave it right there. The answer may come when you least expect it; perhaps in a few minutes, hours, or even days, *but it does come.*

This leads us directly into the next question that was left after the last session. It was, "Who asks the question? What answers the question?"

This is a wonderful question. It shows just how far we have expanded in this Consciousness. The word *questioning* is simply another word for *opening.* When we question, we are just focusing our attention on that particular aspect of existence which concerns us at the moment. This is the only importance of the question. The focusing of our attention reveals the answer that is already present in our own Consciousness.

Why do we ask a specific question? Because the answer to that specific question is *insisting upon revealing itself* right then. Remember, if the answer were not already an eternally established fact, the question would never have been asked.

For instance, if it were not already an eternally established fact that two plus two equals four, no little school child would ever ask the question of what two plus two equals. So we must always remain aware that the answer already exists in our own Consciousness. We use the word *question* because we have to have words. Even so, we realize that all that is taking place is that the answer is already announcing its presence.

We never ask a question of a God outside of, or other than, our own Self. Listening for the answer is the opening of Consciousness in order that the answer may reveal itself. No one would ever be impelled to ask a question unless he knew the answer to that question was already included in his own Consciousness. You know, we have had this thing all turned around. It has seemed that the question came first and was necessary before the answer was realized. Actually, the answer is first, last, and always, and the question only occurs because the answer is, and is as omnipresent as is God Itself.

Of course, you know that no answer is ever revealed from a God outside your own Being. When I first began to ask questions, it seemed to me that I was asking the questions of God, as though He were something outside my Self. Presently I became aware that the answers were not coming from outside my Self at all; I came to realize that the answers were presenting themselves from within my own Consciousness—even to the point that when the answer would be audible, it would be my voice. Yet I had no awareness of having spoken. It was not the voice of Marie Watts; yet I would know that it was the *I* that I am, speaking.

Now let us turn to the revelations of this session. As stated before, there are three steps that we must take in the realization of omnipresent Perfection. It makes no difference whether it is our own perfection we are seeking to perceive or the perfection of one who has asked for help; these three steps are necessary. Actually, it is not a matter of taking progressive steps at all but rather a matter of expanding revelation. But this expanding revelation must reveal the nature of the Universe, the nature of the Identity, and the nature of the Body. Why? Because they are all One, as you will discover during this class.

The subject of the first session was, "What is the nature of the Universe?" Now let us ask another question: "Why is the Universe? Why do stars, planets, galaxies exist?"

The answer is simple: God *must* express Itself. An unexpressed God is inconceivable. God must express Himself. There is no such thing as an unexpressed God. There is no such thing as an unidentified God. God is not a purposeless God. Really, it wouldn't be intelligent for God to be a purposeless God.

Each one of us has a purpose in being. If we glimpse this but dimly, we will see that God must have a purpose in being and must eternally and infinitely fulfill that purpose. God does fulfill His purpose in being by the expression of Himself. There can be no such thing as God failing to fulfill His purpose in being. The stars, the planets, the galaxies are evidence of the fact that God *is*. God's evidence of Himself is manifested as the Substance, the Form, and the orderly, intelligent Activity of the heavenly bodies and the Universe. "The heavens declare the glory of God" (Ps. 19:20). This is a wonderful and glorious truth to realize. All that exists is God evidencing Itself as the Infinite All; but God is also manifesting Itself as each specific Identity that is essential to His completeness *as* the Infinite All.

What evidence that God exists would there be if there were no such thing as Substance, Form, and Activity? What evidence would there be that God is Life if there were no Substance or Form to manifest Life? There has to be evidence of that which exists. If there were no Substance in Form, there would be no way in which Life, Activity, would be evident.

Before there can be activity, there must be something that is active. Indeed, there *is* Something that is active, and this Something is not matter. It has Form, Substance, Life, and Activity, but It is entirely comprised of God, Spirit, Consciousness, Life Itself. There is no use in saying, "God is All" unless we are perceiving that *God is the entirety of the Universe Itself.* How can we be misled by the illusion that the bodies of the stars and planets are matter, when we know that God really is All? God is completely and entirely Spirit, Mind, Life, Love, and far more than all the synonyms could represent.

Indeed, there is Form. There is Substance in Form, but the Form is not material. The Substance in Form is not matter. There is no matter. We explore this subject more fully in the next session. All that has been said in this session pertaining to God as the Universe has been for the purpose of maintaining the continuity of these sessions.

Now let us turn to the second step in the realization of Perfection: *What is the Identity?*

The answer to this question may be stated very simply and in just a few words. *God is the Identity of everyone and everyone in existence.* It is as simple as that. Yet it somehow isn't enough to just say this and stop there. It is too simple. Yet it is the Ultimate Truth. But it isn't specific enough. That is the seeming difficulty most students of the Absolute are having in the realization of Perfection. It is true that God is All; but this isn't going to help you much if you seem to have some specific problem and you do not know what God is as the answer to that specific problem.

Why must we be specific? Because each one of us is a specific Identity. Each Identity — no matter what may be the specific nature of that Identity — is a distinct Identity and no other. Each star, each planet, each leaf, and each blade of grass is that specific Identity. This is the reason we should be specific in the Truth we see and know. The Truth is identified as each specific Identity and should be perceived as that specific Identity. This specific "seeing," however, does not mean that God, Truth, is divided or separated in Its expression of Its Allness. God,

infinite Consciousness, is eternally One and inseparable. Yet this same God is eternally identified as an
infinite variety of specific identities.

It doesn't help very much to say, "God is the
specific Identity" unless we know what God is.
When we really *know* what God is, we can then
know what God is as each specific Identity.
Omnipresence means God being equally present
everywhere and always.

First of all, God is Itself. This statement may, at
first glance, appear superfluous. But closer attention
will reveal that it is of tremendous importance to
perceive that God is Itself. All is God, and God is
Itself as All. So it is of the greatest importance to
realize that God is Itself, no matter what is revealed
as the specific nature of that Identity. No matter
what the specific Identity may be named or mis-
named, it still is God being Itself as that distinct
Identity.

You will remember that in the first session we
spoke of the unbounded revelation through the
contemplation of the heavens. You will also
remember that we at least caught a glimpse of God
as the infinite, unrestricted, spaceless, timeless
nature of the Universe. God, identified, must be all
that God is, identified. So it is that God, identifying
Itself as the specific Identity that you are and the
specific Identity that I am, remains unlimited,
unrestricted, spaceless, timeless, infinite, eternal
Life, Love, Truth, Mind, Consciousness—in fact, all

that God is. Isn't that wonderful! *All that God is, eternally and without interruption, is identified as your specific Identity.* This means that all that God *is* constitutes all that you *are.*

God does not identify Itself in partials or in parts. There is no such thing as a little bit of God identified as one of us, a little bit of God as another, and a lot of God identified as someone more fortunate. All that God is, is identified wherever God expresses and identifies Itself. And this means everywhere, without a vacuum, without an interruption.

Do you see what this means? It means absolute freedom. It means that the Identity that you are this very instant is unconfined, unlimited, unrestricted, free, and consciously perfect. You are not limited by the fallacy called "time" to a certain number of years of Life. You are not limited to a certain degree of joy, of happiness; you are not limited to a degree of health, to a little bit of wealth, to a certain amount of success and fulfillment. You are not limited to a few dollars a week or a month. You are not limited to a certain degree of Love. How can you be? You are complete health, abundance, Love, and Life Itself identified. How can you be subject to these spurious limitations? *You are not.*

All that God is, is identified as each one of you. You are just waking up. *You are at the standpoint of discovering what you really are.* You are just beginning to really feel and experience the complete joy, freedom, and perfection that you eternally are. Oh, my friends, if you really see and feel this Truth, you will find yourselves experiencing more and more of the unrestricted, unlimited freedom and joy that you are right now seeing and feeling.

Now do you see the importance of contemplating the infinitude of the heavens? Do you perceive how important this revelation is to the realization of your own freedom, of your own eternal, infinite joy and completeness? The silent contemplation of the boundless peace and perfection of the heavens invariably reveals the boundless and unlimited peace and perfection that *you* are.

Of course, you might question, "Freedom from what?" And the answer would be: freedom from every fallacy that would seem to bind or limit you — freedom from fear and anxiety; freedom from pain, from illness; freedom from birth, the pains of childhood; freedom from the claims of age, the claim of death. Dear friends, this means freedom from everything that is not God; thus, freedom from everything that is not God being you. This is the freedom you realize. Yes, all this and much more do you realize as the full, spiritual significance of this infinite God-Universe reveals Itself to be your eternal Being.

So much of our seeming difficulty stems from the fact that we measure our experience from that which is called birth to that which is called death. So often we say, "It takes such a long time to get this understanding." How often we have said it.

These false limitations of time disappear when we once perceive the eternality of our Being and are fully aware that each one of us, as an individual, has always existed, will always continue to exist. When we see that we, as individuals, are without beginning, without change, and without interruptions, we cease to be concerned about this fallacy called time. We realize that all of the so-called years between birth and death are but a pinpoint in the infinitude that is the Universe. We get a perspective of how rapidly we are becoming aware of what we really are when we see it in this way.

So when something seems to be troublesome, it is always well to remember the infinite, eternal nature of your Being. This is particularly true when some false claim seems to continue to present itself for what seems to be a long period of time. Always measure the "time" of your seeming trouble in terms of your eternality. If you persist in this *seeing*, you will realize that this so-called time of trouble is but a pinpoint in your eternal Being, and soon you will discover that even the pinpoint is not genuine and has no existence.

No revelation of the infinite All-existence would be complete unless God, expressed and identified as infinite, eternal Beauty, were realized. God is Beauty. Without God there would be no Beauty. It is also true that without Beauty there would be no

God. *God can only identify Itself as what God is.* You are God identified. God is infinite, eternal Beauty. The Beauty that is God is identified—so you are Beauty. You exist as the Beauty that is God. The fact that you exist as an Identity at all means that you exist as Beauty.

Here we are going right back to the fundamental fact that *all* of God is identified as each Identity. God is Beauty, so He must be identified as Beauty. In knowing that you are just what God is—and nothing else—you are aware that *you are Beauty.* Knowing also that your Consciousness is your Universe, can you be aware of any ugliness in your Universe? Can there be an ugly situation in your environment? Can there be anything sordid or obnoxious in your Universe? Your Consciousness is your Universe; your Consciousness is Beauty; so all that exists as your Universe is beautiful.

Right now someone is asking a question. Yes, I hear the question just as well as if it were audible. Your question is, "But there are several Identities in this room. Does this mean that each Identity in this room is my Consciousness?"

Indeed it does. We are inseparably one Consciousness. But this does not mean that you, as an Identity, can possibly displace another Identity. Neither can you usurp the Identity of another Identity. Remember, we are not talking about dense, solid, or obstructive matter. *There is no matter.* We are speaking of Consciousness.

Let me illustrate it in this way. I am conscious of the fact that I am Life; I am aware that I am Beauty; I am aware of the fact that I am conscious Mind, Intelligence. Yet you, also, are fully aware that you are all of these aspects of Life. My awareness of my Identity cannot usurp your awareness of your Identity. Yet I am aware of you; thus, you are included in my Universe. You are my Consciousness because my Consciousness is my Universe. You are conscious of me, thus, I am included in your Universe. Because your Consciousness is your Universe, I am your Consciousness.

This, of course, is another way of saying that God, identified as your Consciousness and as my Consciousness, is the same God. Yes, the same Consciousness but specifically identified as your Identity and as my Identity.

Let us return to the aspect of God that is Beauty. There is tremendous power in the realization that your Consciousness is Beauty and that your Consciousness is Perfection. This realization discloses that Beauty and Perfection are all that is included in your Universe. This truth is no mere theory. It has proven itself to be true and will prove itself to be true in your practical affairs.

For instance, let me share with you a recent experience in which this truth proved itself. A friend (who is here at this session) and I were driving northward to San Francisco. When we were a few miles south of Bakersfield, we were flagged to a stop by a highway patrolman, who told us that we would have to detour. We were informed that in the dense fog, several cars had collided, blocking the road. We detoured, and certain it is that we could see dense fog on both sides of the highways.

Mile after mile we drove, aware of the seemingly impenetrable fog at some distance away on either side of the road. But here is the important point: not for one instant were we aware of any fog on the highway, Right in the midst of that seeming fog, here was this beautiful road, like a ribbon, stretching out before us. All was perfectly clear as far as we could see in the distance. Even in the distance there was no sign of fog on the highway. It was a glorious experience.

Now, the question is: what did we see? What did we realize that was so powerful that even a dense blanket of fog could be seen through and the perfectly beautiful highway be seen all through the experience? We saw that our Consciousness is our Universe. We knew that there was no fog in or as our Consciousness; thus there was no fog in our Universe. That beautiful, clear highway was an essential aspect of our Consciousness just then, so that perfectly, clear highway was manifested right where our Consciousness was focused at the moment. I cannot stress enough the importance of realizing that God, Beauty, Perfection, is your Consciousness; and your Consciousness is your Universe.

Beauty and Perfection are one and the same thing. We hear of the "beauty of perfection." How often we say, "Why, that is perfectly beautiful." Haven't you heard that statement? I have. It is really surprising how we use certain words together and thereby express a genuine spiritual truth. You see, the actuality—that which really exists—does shine through; yes, it shows right through the so-called dream. This is evident in the way we connect words; we say, "perfectly beautiful," or, "the beauty of perfection."

We often say of someone, "Isn't she perfectly lovely!" Right here we have used the word *love* to designate Perfection and Beauty. Love *is* beauty. Perfection *is* Beauty. Love *is* Perfection. "Perfect love casteth out fear" (1 John 4:18). Also it is said that we are "made perfect in love." This is true and right, because Love, Beauty, Perfection are not separate, they are One, and this One is God expressed, identified.

How often we speak of the love between two individuals as being beautiful. I have seen such love, and I thought it was beautiful. I have experienced it, and do experience it, and I know it is beautiful. So you see, even in the seeming dream, we are more aware of Truth than we sometimes realize.

Yes, Beauty is Perfection. Perfection is Beauty. God, as Beauty, Perfection, is identified as the Beauty of Perfection that is your Identity, This Beauty of Perfection that is God is identified as the

Beauty, the Perfection that is your Consciousness. Your Consciousness is your Universe; so your Universe is perfectly beautiful and beautifully perfect.

As we contemplate the heavens, particularly at night, we are impressed with the beautiful Perfection revealed throughout the Universe. I am aware that there is some question among our friends, the physicists, as to whether or not the Universe is perfect. There are some very advanced physicists who contend that the Universe is probably perfect. Others contend that it is imperfect. You will remember that a few years ago the physicists believed that the stars, planets, and galaxies had no order in their arrangement or in their movement. They thought that they were just drifting about in a haphazard manner. Through more recent investigations, they have discovered that there is perfect order in the heavens. Of course they would have to discover that there is perfect order in the heavens because the Universe Itself is God, infinite, eternal Perfection.

Why does the Universe appear to be imperfect to some physicists? It is because they are attempting to discover and to analyze the Universe from the standpoint of matter. As there is no matter, the entire basis of their analysis is faulty; and of course the manifestation would appear to be imperfect. Viewed from a false premise, the only conclusion to be found is false and the manifestation imperfect.

There is no such thing as perfect matter. There is no matter to be either perfect or imperfect.

This is a good thing to remember when we are tempted to look to what appears to be matter for results. There cannot be Perfection manifested in matter, for Perfection is Spirit, God. There is no matter, so we don't look to matter to see perfect results or manifestations. In fact, we don't look for results at all because we know that all is already perfect. This does not mean that we do not realize Perfection. Indeed, we do; but we know that this Perfection is not perfect matter. It might look as if it were matter to John Jones down the street, but we know it is not matter. In the next session, we are going to discover just exactly what does exist right here instead of matter.

There is just no use going around denying and denying that there is Substance in Form. And why do some of our friends along this path deny the Body? We don't deny that the planets are bodies. Even the astronomers speak of the "bodies of the planets." They also call this Earth planet a body. We certainly don't deny that which is called the Earth body; why, then, should we deny that there is Substance in Form as our Bodies? Let us freely admit that there is Something here in Form, that this Something is Substance and that this Substance in Form is the Body. Then let us discover what this Something is that is here as the Body.

The Universe is perfect *now*. God is the Universe and God is Perfection. God can only identify Itself as what God is. So God must identify Itself as a perfect Universe. If this were not true, God would have to identify Itself as something that God is not. This cannot be. Even God cannot identify Itself as that which It is not. God must identify Itself as perfect stars, perfect planets, and perfect galaxies. God must identify Itself as the perfect Order and Activity that is apparent as the orderly movement, the universal Order, and the Activity that is revealed as the perfect Universe.

You are God identified. The complete Perfection which is God must, and does, identify Itself. It identifies Itself as completeness. The complete Perfection which is God identifies Itself as the complete Perfection which is you.

Right here, I must clarify my use of the word *you*. In expressing Truth, we have to use words. I cannot address you without making use of the word *you*. But the use of this word does not mean that I regard you as a person. Neither does it mean that I see you as an individual or as an identity separate and apart from the one *I*, which is God. The word *you* means God identified, just as the word *I* means God identified. God identified as the one *I* means the one *you*, the One only, which I address by the use of the word *you*. There is no *you* but God; there is no *I* but God.

69

Now, let us return to our subject. The complete Perfection which is God is the complete Perfection which comprises all there is of you. This complete Perfection means so very much. It means that you are perfect as Substance. It means that you are perfect as Form, Life, Activity. How could it be otherwise, when God is all that exists as Substance, Form, Life, and Activity. It means that you are perfect in every function. Ponder the stars and planets again. Think of their perfect, beautiful Order, their perfect, orderly Activity, their perfect functioning.

Dear friends, don't you see that this is the very same Power, the same Perfection that is functioning as you—as your entire Life and Activity? Yes, this realization of complete Perfection means much. It means that your affairs, your experiences, your relationships are completely perfect. It means that your entire experience is entirely perfect because Perfection has to express Itself *as* Perfection. Complete Perfection has to *express* Itself as complete Perfection. Completeness cannot express Itself as incompleteness. Perfection cannot express Itself as imperfection.

Order cannot express itself as disorder. This means that there is complete, perfect Order in your daily experience and in your Body. It makes no difference what your daily affairs may be—whether you are in business, a profession, keeping a home, whatever—there is perfect, complete Order manifesting Itself as your experience. And it is the same omnipotent Order that we observe in the movement of the stars and planets. Here there is not a single mistake, not a single deviation from this perfect Order. No planet moves out of its orbit. No indeed; each star and planet is right where it should be, when it should be there, doing exactly what it should be doing, when it should be doing it. And this is not a bad lesson for us to learn.

I believe that each one of you will be more aware of the Universe. I believe that you are going to measure each experience by the Perfection that is evident as this Universe. And I believe that if your experience doesn't measure up to this universal Perfection, you are going to dwell in Consciousness on the complete Perfection that is the Universe, until you perceive that this Perfection really is going on in and as your daily experience. Always remember this: the Identity that you are right now is the same Principle in complete, perfect operation that is functioning as the Activity of the entire Universe right now. It is the same Principle governing Itself. It is not Principle governing you as if you were something other than Itself. Rather it is Principle governing Itself *as* you.

We need to be careful here; we must realize that it is not Principle governing a star or a planet as if it were something other than Itself. The Mind, the Principle, *is* the Substance, Activity, and Form of the planet It is governing. So it is with you. This Principle, Mind, Life, Consciousness is the very

Substance that comprises you. Thus, It is governing Itself *as* you. God is the Principle that governs Itself. God governs Itself as the orderly movement of the heavenly bodies. It holds Itself as these bodies in perfect order and in their lovely relationship to each other.

We cannot leave Love out of the Universe. Without Love there would be no Universe. Without Love there would be no harmony, no order. What is it that holds the stars and planets in such beautiful harmony with each other? *Love!* It is Love that attracts; it is Love that holds; it is Love that is power. Unless you know and feel that you are Love, you are not completely aware of what you really are.

God is the Principle identified as the Identity that you are. The perfect Principle loses none of Its Power and Perfection because It is identified as you, or as your Identity. Does Principle become any less Principle because It is you? No! It remains omnipotent. It remains complete in the fullness of Its Perfection. It remains Its own eternal, changeless Self, identified as your Self.

You are not even responsible for the operation of this Principle. Is any one of the stars or planets responsible for its own operation, separate and apart from the one All-Principle in action? Could any one of them operate of itself and independently? Has any one of them power and intelligence to do anything or to be anything, separate and apart from God? No! If any heavenly body could have power of its own, independent of Omnipotence, we would have chaos in the heavens. Not one of the stars or planets is responsible for its own activity—not even for its own existence. Neither is any star or planet responsible for the existence or activity of another star or planet. Neither are you responsible for the existence or the activity of another Identity.

It is well to consider every universal truth as the truth of your own experience. This is the big lesson for all of us. *Principle, Mind, is responsible for Itself.* Principle, identified as your Identity, is governing Itself as your entire existence. This means that Principle is governing Itself as your Life, your affairs, your experience, your Body, and as your Being.

*Principle is not governing you as if you were something other than Itself.* It is always Principle governing Itself *as* your Self. Principle does not make mistakes. Principle is Mind (Intelligence) and cannot have an awareness of mistakes. Principle, governing Itself as your Self, maintains Itself in constant, perfect, harmonious Activity. It holds Itself in perfect Order. It keeps Itself in perfect relationship as every other Identity in your Universe. There is no Identity in your Universe that is not the same God Consciousness that you are. Principle maintains Itself in Its perfect, orderly Activity as every Identity in your Universe. No Identity in your Universe can get out of Its right spiritual orbit. Neither can It act or function in any way opposite or contrary to the

Principle which is governing Itself as that specific Identity.

This is a very good point to remember in driving a car. It isn't enough to know that God is keeping Itself in perfect order as your activity. It is also essential to know that Principle is holding Itself in Its perfect order, in Its proper orbit, as every other driver and every other One in your Universe. It is well to know that Principle moves Itself without mistakes, that It knows no deviation and no interruption in Its perfect Activity. It is important to perceive that Principle governing Itself is never interrupted. Sometimes it seems that there are interruptions, but God does not interrupt Itself. Neither does God interrupt Itself as you—as your experience or as your Consciousness, which is your Universe.

Do you see what we are doing now? We are beginning to realize that God, the Perfection that governs Itself as the Universe, is the Principle that governs Itself as you. *Principle is Intelligence.* When we speak the word *Mind*, I always consider It to be Intelligence. I do not use the word *Mind* from the standpoint of thinking or reasoning. If there were such a thing as a thinking or reasoning mind, it would indicate that God was not supreme, All-knowing Intelligence right now. This would mean that Mind had to take time to think or to reason out Its own answers, It is the so-called thinking mind that is supposed to have a memory. A human mind that remembers can seem to remember many things it would rather forget. All of us know that this is true. This is the reason I don't deal with the word *memory*. This is also why I only speak of Mind in referring to Intelligence.

I like the word *Consciousness*. Consciousness has nothing to do with thought or reasoning. Consciousness requires no time in order to become conscious. Consciousness is awareness, and awareness is right here and right now. Instead of saying *mind*, which is supposed to have a very unhappy faculty of memory, with a time element for reasoning or thinking, let us say *Consciousness*, which means omnipresent Awareness.

Principle is Mind; Mind is Intelligence. Mind and Principle are the same thing, so Principle is intelligent. Therefore, the Omnipotence that controls Itself as the Activity of the Universe is an intelligent Power. Indeed It is. It is Intelligence in action. This intelligent Power knows Itself to be the Universe. It controls Itself as the Universe. This is the reason the Activity that goes on in the heavens is so perfect. Intelligence *does* govern. It governs as intelligent government. Mind does not govern anything separate or other than Itself. There isn't anything existing outside of, or other than, the Self-government that is Mind, Intelligence, in action. In short, there isn't any action other than Intelligence in action. This Intelligence in action is Mind, governing Itself intelligently. Now, where and when are there any mistakes? They just aren't; they do not exist and they never happen.

This Activity is Perfection in action. Mind does govern, but It does not govern anything separate or other than Itself. Mind, Intelligence, is the very Substance—even the Substance in form called the Body—of that which It intelligently governs. Mind, Intelligence, is the only Substance of the Form which It is governing. It is also the Form of the Substance which It governs. This is the Activity which is omnipresent, omniactive, as your Body and as the Body of everyone.

The very same Intelligence, as you, is also governing Itself as the Activity of the stars and planets. It is intelligently active as your Identity. It does not weaken. It does not relinquish Its omnipotent, intelligent government just because It is identified as you. Dear friends, *it is because It is identified as you that It can fulfill Its purpose as Intelligence in action.*

How often we have said that if there were no God, there would be no Identity. But do we know that if there were no Identity, there would be no God? *You are essential. Each specific Identity is essential in order that God be complete.* The Intelligence that is God in action as your Identity is essential in order that God be complete Intelligence in orderly Activity. You, as a person, are not responsible for your own intelligence in action. You *are* intelligent Activity. You are God, intelligently active, experiencing Itself. Can you see how far we have to go when we say, "God is All"? *We have to go all the way.*

Mind is responsible for Itself. It is responsible for Itself as you. Intelligence is responsible for being intelligent as your intelligence. With this realization, you can really let go. You can really cease all human struggling or striving. You can depend upon this Intelligence. You can depend upon the Mind that is identified as your intelligence to act intelligently as you. You can depend upon the Mind that is the Intelligence, identified as everyone in your Universe, to act intelligently as each Identity that is active in your Universe. You are aware that it is the same Intelligence governing Itself as you that is governing Itself as the Identity of each Identity in your Universe.

It may be someone in a car; it may be a salesman at the door or in a store; it may be your neighbor or a friend; it may also be someone who says that you have opinions that lack intelligence. It doesn't make any difference. You are not concerned about that. Your only concern is just to keep right on realizing that Intelligence in action is governing Itself as you and as everything and everyone in your Universe. You don't accept or pay any attention to anything or anyone who *appears* to be acting unintelligently.

If you continue in this Consciousness, presently you will discover that you are no longer even *seeming* to have experiences with others that are inharmonious. This is because your own God Consciousness manifests Itself as your Universe. Then you discover that when you walk into a store, a cafe, or along the street, the troubled faces you meet light up with a glad smile. You have seen this happen. So have I, and we will have this joyous experience increasingly.

Does this mean that we do nothing? No, indeed it does not! Quite the contrary; we are intensely, joyously alive and active. We do whatever is before us to do. But the work, the struggle, and the strain are not to be found in this joyous activity.

Not long ago I talked with someone who did not wish to work. Her theory was that work is unneces sary. She said, "I don't believe that it is right to work for a living." Then she came forth with that old, overworked statement, "Man was not meant to till the soil." All of us know that it was Adam who was sentenced to "till the soil." We also know that we are not the offspring of Adam. But we often hear someone twisting the truth pertaining to these statements, in order to do just what he wants to do and no more or less.

Of course, I agree with the statement that we need not work for a living. However, this does not mean that we are idle, unemployed. Total idleness would be total inactivity. That would be death—the opposite of Life. Life is ever purposefully active, because Life is Activity. There is no such thing as an inactive God. God is Life. Life is Activity. There is no such thing as a purposeless God. God in constant action is God fulfilling Its purpose in being. God in action is your activity, is God actively fulfilling Its purpose in being you. Of course it is right that we work, that we be active. Just as God actively fulfills Its purpose by identifying Itself as you, so it is that your activity is God in action, identified as your activity.

Indeed, we are active. We are the fulfillment of God's purpose in being active as each one of us. This whole belief that we must "till the soil," work for a living, belongs in the category of the illusion. It is the illusion's misinterpretation of activity as well as being the mistaken sense of supply. In this misinterpretation, it seems that everything must be done with an effort, that all work must be labor. This is just another aspect of the illusion that we can do something, be something, of ourselves, separate and apart from God.

This falsity includes the accompanying delusion that our supply is somewhere separate and apart from us, that we have to do something of ourselves in order to bring this supply into our experience. However, when we realize that we have no responsibility of ourselves, for ourselves, separate from God, but that God is responsible for Itself as our Identity and experience, we are no longer concerned with working for a living.

Let God fulfill Its purpose in being you. Let that Mind actually be your Mind. It already *is* your

Mind; let It *be*. God is the Intelligence that knows Itself to be the Supply for the fulfillment of Its every purpose. Be not concerned about making a living. Be not concerned about bringing *in* Supply. God is conscious of being all there is of you, including all that is essential to your completeness. Supply is essential to your completeness, so God is conscious of being your Supply, as your Consciousness of your own Supply. It would be impossible for you to exist unless you included the Supply that is essential to your completeness. You could not know the truth you know—you could not even be conscious and fail to be aware of the Supply that is already included in your completeness. You would not be complete if you did not include the Supply that is necessary to your existence.

Being active is another matter. You are active because you are Activity. But it isn't labor, and it isn't "working to make a living." You have to be active if you are alive because you are alive as Life (Activity) Itself. God is Omniaction, and God identifies Itself as just what God is and nothing else. Activity cannot identify Itself as inactivity. You are God identified. You know that you are something. Indeed, you *are* Something, and that Something is God in perfect action right now.

You are just what God is in action. Your Activity is God, *Omniaction*, identifying Itself as your Activity. God is Mind, Intelligence, so all Activity is intelligent Activity. You are Intelligence in action.

This is the reason your Activity is always perfect, orderly, and fruitful. This is the reason there is no struggle, strain, or effort in your Activity.

You exist as the very presence of the Power that governs Itself as the Universe. This Power acts as your Activity. How can you become exhausted? How can you be frustrated or confused in your Activity? How can you fail in the fulfillment of your purpose in being active? You can't. You don't. How can there be unintelligent Activity? How can Intelligence Itself be active and not act intelligently?

There is no indication that the Activity of the stars and planets is labored or strained. There is no indication that there is any confusion, exhaustion, frustration, or failure in the Activity of the heavenly bodies. If God can and does govern and maintain Itself without strain as the Universe, cannot God govern and maintain Itself perfectly as the Activity of the Identity that you are? Indeed He can, and does, when you stop this thing of feeling falsely responsible for yourself as a mortal or human being.

You will remember that Jesus said, "I must be about my Father's business" (Luke 2:49). Who, or what, is the *I* that must be about the Father's business? The *I* is the Father Itself being about Its own business.

We have always been taught that God spoke *to* Moses, Jeremiah, and the prophets. We have been told that God spoke *to* Jesus, Paul, and the disciples. We have also believed that God could speak *to* us.

There is not one particle of truth in that belief. *Every word of truth that has ever been spoken has been God Itself speaking that Word as the Identity hearing it*. Even though the Word was spoken by the identities named Jeremiah, Isaiah, or Jesus, it was God Itself revealing Its own truth as the very Identity that was speaking the truth.

There was, there is, the eternal Identity that was called (for a split second in his eternal being) by the name of Jesus. God spoke *as* that Identity. God did not speak *to* Jesus. God did not even speak *through* Jesus. God speaks as God and none other. Wherever Truth appears, it is God appearing as that Truth. This is an important point to remember. *There is no chosen one to whom God speaks. God is equally God as each Identity in existence.* Every word of Truth you speak is God speaking *as* you. This is the reason the Truth is omnipotent. Only God can know and speak the word of Truth.

I am sure of this. Let me tell you why I am so sure that this is true. It is because I know how the book *The Ultimate* and the booklets were written. I know that God did not reveal the words of Truth in *The Ultimate* or any of the other books *to* me. I know that it was God revealing His own Truth, expressing Himself, identified as the "*I* that I am." Those words were not spoken to or through a little person named Marie. In fact, it was not until it was realized that there was no person named Marie that God spoke as the *I* that I am. I know, beyond a doubt, that God reveals Itself *as* Itself and not to or through a person.

Let us return to that statement, "I must be about my Father's business." *I*—the *I* that I am—must be busy too. The *I* that is identified as you must also be busy. Why? Because the Father, identified as the *I* that I am and identified as the *I* that you are, is busy *as* your business and *as* my business. And it is all the Father's business, for there is none other.

The Bible also states, "My Father worketh hitherto, and I work" (John 5:17). God works; God is active; God *is* Activity. The *I* that I am is always about Its business. I couldn't stop being active if I tried. Neither could you. How could we? Could we resist God, who is our very existence? Who or what exists who could oppose the irresistible, irrepressible Life that is God?

Jesus knew that God was his *only* Identity. He knew that of himself he could do nothing. He knew that of himself he was nothing. But he also knew that, as God identified, his work was God revealing Its own perfect Activity. He knew that God was the *only* one doing the work.

What was the work? Was it healing? No! God is infinite Intelligence, all Power, all Presence; God *is* All; All *is* God. Thus, all is Perfection because God *is* Perfection. An all-powerful, all-perfect, God—knowing Itself to be All—would not send His son to heal or correct mistakes that He had made or had permitted to happen. What was God's purpose in

83

appearing as the one named Jesus? It was to disperse the myth of the dreamer, to announce His Presence and Power to be All as All. It was, and is, God revealing and evidencing His Perfection to be All, His Power to be All, as All that exists of any one of us.

"The Father that dwelleth in me, he doeth the works" (John 14:10). Yes, my Father lives as the very Life that is alive as my eternal, changeless, perfect Life and as your eternal, changeless, perfect Life. "He doeth the works." Well, what does it matter whether the so-called personal name be John, Mary, or any other name, it is still God doing Its work, fulfilling Its own purpose *as* you, *as* your work.

Again, Jesus knew that of himself he could do nothing, be nothing. But he also knew that as the very presence of God identified, he could do all because he knew that he was Omnipotence in action. This is also true of us. We are amazed at what we can do when we *know* what we are—when we know who is doing the work as our specific Identity.

Let us return to the word *contemplation*. As I stated before, I do not think or reason my way into contemplation; it is not a thought process. I cannot present you with a formula for this activity. Each one of us must discover his own way. So when you engage in contemplation, please do not use exact words. Remember, all of the Truth that is ever going to be revealed as your own Being must be revealed from within your own Consciousness.

*You are the Truth yourself,* so do not use any words other than those which are revealed from within your own Being. In fact, I find that the words that come when I enter contemplation are seldom, if ever, the same words. Truth is ever new and fresh, and It always reveals Itself in and as words that are new and fresh. This is why It is always so inspiring. However, I am saying these words because it may help you to discover your own way and in your own words.

First I sit quietly. As I have stated before, for some reason I feel that my Consciousness is more open when my palms are up. I don't know why this should be true. I don't deliberately do this; I just discover that my hands are in this position. I don't really think that the position of the hands has anything to do with it. But somehow I find that in the complete surrender of that which has claimed to be a personal self, my hands are open with the palms up. Then I say something like this:

> "I thank you, my God-Being—all there is of me—that of myself I can do nothing; of myself I can know nothing; of myself I can be nothing because of myself I am nothing."

Then I rest in this Consciousness until I am sure that there is no little false dream-person calling herself "Marie" trying to think or to reason. Not until all false sense of the little "I" is obliterated is it *possible* for me to claim my Identity in His name—in the name of the Almighty God, I AM. Then, and only then, can I say, "I thank you, my God-Being, the *I* that I am, that I am just what You are as Me—and nothing else."

Now that all false personal sense is obliterated, I find that I am in contemplation. My attention can now be fully occupied in perceiving all that God is. This is a glorious experience and one that cannot be described. If there seems to be some specific need, I then focus my attention upon the truth pertaining to that *specific* situation. I never dwell on the need. Why should I? It isn't present anyway. I am too aware that all is God to be aware of any need. But I am specific in perceiving God to be the Truth instead of the false appearance of any specific fallacy calling itself a human need.

For instance, if the *seeming* need should be for perfect activity, I focus my complete attention on God as *all* Activity. I perceive that God, being active, is purposefully active and that God is fulfilling His purpose perfectly as that specific function or activity. I perceive God to be Omnipotence in perfect, unopposed, omnipotent Activity—as the functioning of the heavenly bodies, as the functioning of that which is called the Earth planet, and as the Body of the specific Identity who has called for help. This does not involve a formula at all. I just feel full open and let God reveal Itself as It will, as this specific aspect of Its Allness.

You can see how this same approach would operate if the illusion seemed to have something to do with the substance of the Body, the daily business affairs, or with supply. It makes no difference what the falsity seems to be; it is well to perceive just what God is, as that particular aspect of Itself, and then to be specific in this perception.

This activity is without labor, struggle, or strain. Above all, it is fruitful activity. It is purposeful activity. Never dawdle in this work. Be fully aware that there is a definite purpose in this activity, and this purpose is to perceive the truth of this particular situation. *It is never to heal, to change, or improve a condition.* There is no purposeless activity. *All is God,* and all activity is purposeful. All activity is fruitful because all activity is God fulfilling His purpose in being active. All activity is God in action, fulfilling His own function, fulfilling His own purpose. So there is no purposeless activity.

Being active in this way, we no longer appear to be faced with frustration, delay, or failure. In fact, we cannot help but realize fruition and success. God is never aware of a delay. God knows no such thing as a failure to accomplish His purpose. There are not "yet four months, and then cometh the harvest" (John 4:35). The harvest *is*—the fruition is *right now.* The activity would not be complete unless the fruition were one with the activity. The fulfillment of the purpose of the activity has to be simultaneous with the activity because the activity and the fruition are one complete entirety.

Why do we seem to experience disappointments and delays? It is because the little personal "I" is attempting to do something. This non-identity is attempting to be something of itself, to usurp God's Power, God's Activity, to be something of itself other than God. That is why we seem to have frustrations, failures, or delays in the full realization of Perfection.

When we *know* that of ourselves we are nothing, when we know that it is God who worketh in us, *as* us, both to will and to do His own good and fruitful work, we discover, even as did Jesus, that there is no struggle, no delay, and no failure.

We also find that there is no attempt to usurp the place of another, no imposition by one upon another, no mad ambition to attain, to prove, to claim the power of the glory that is God Itself in action. None of these little personal falsities has anything to do with omnipotent Intelligence in action. None of these fallacies have anything to do with God fulfilling Its purpose in being active *as* your activity.

There is a great humility that flows through, in, and as your Consciousness when you realize that of yourself you are nothing. Then you are fully aware of how futile it would be to claim to be able to help or to heal anything. You are so very aware that there is only God; that He is not in need of help or healing, and if He were, you could do nothing about it at all, for of yourself you are nothing. You really feel about the size of a pinpoint, and presently even the pinpoint disappears.

When this takes place, there is a great surge of pure ecstasy as you perceive that it is only because God is All that you exist; it is only because God sees that you can see; it is only because God acts that you can act; and it is only because God *is* that you can *be*. In this great humility, there is a tremendous power.

It is in this humility that you suddenly realize that you are as infinite as is the Universe. You know that you are infinite Power, infinite Intelligence, infinite Love and Life, infinite Consciousness being. When we know that it is God who worketh *as* us to do His own good pleasure, we see the utter futility of all little personal effort to do or be anything. We see how senseless is all this pushing, pulling, or elbowing of another or imposing upon another. We see how utterly futile is the mad ambition to attain power or position over another — to attempt to usurp the business, the activities, the opportunity of another. There is no desire to attain leadership, to have a following, or even to try to be the Christ for other individuals. All of this illusion is obliterated. We are just too busy knowing our God-Being to be aware of all this so-called world of sense — which is *non*sense.

Now we have arrived at this important question: why do we have an Identity? Why do we exist as the specific Identity that is conscious as our distinct Identity?

We exist as a specific Identity because God must fulfill Its purpose. God must express Itself. God must present the evidence of Itself as just what It is. God is Its own Identity. God is infinite Identity. Within the Infinitude that is God, the infinite Identity, there are infinite Identities. The word *infinite* means innumerable, as well as spaceless or boundless. This infinite variety is essential to God's complete expression of Its infinite, beautiful nature.

Wouldn't it be dull, wouldn't it be boring, if there were no variety? Suppose there were only one color; suppose all food tasted the same; suppose there were only one tone or pitch in music; or, for that matter, suppose that each one of us were exactly the same in appearance. True, the *appearance* is not the Identity, but it does give us an inkling of the fact that no two Identities are exact duplicates. Every Identity in this Universe is a specific Identity—but every Identity in this Universe is God identified as Itself.

Let us explore this infinite variety of Identities in which God expresses and identifies Itself. Here we must always remember one important point: God does not separate or divide Itself from Itself in Its expression and identification of Itself. Never lose sight of the fact that the one Infinite All is never divided. But God does identify Itself as innumerable expressions of Itself.

There is one more important point that we must always remember: we are not speaking of persons, mortals, solid masses with space dimensions, or of nonexistent matter in any guise. God identified is Spirit, not matter. God identified is not a mortal, a material animal or object. God identified is God revealing Itself and nothing else.

Now to continue: The infinite variety of God's expressions of Itself is evident in an infinite variety of specific expressions. The species called man could be considered as a specific expression of God. This is also true of the species called animal, fish, or fowl. Then there is the species called tree, flower, plant, and innumerable other specific expressions of the one Infinite All. But within each specific expression, there is an infinite variety of specific expressions or identities. This is an interesting Universe, and variety is essential to Its completeness. Life is inspiring and interesting. Life couldn't be alive if It were not vitally interesting. Life would not be inspiring or interesting if there were no variety. This variety is necessary in order that God reveal Itself as *all that It is.*

God is all existence. God is all of the variety. God is every Identity included in the variety. God is every variety, every Identity. The variation in form, in color, in identities is essential in order that all of the varieties that God is may be expressed and identified, "for all shall know me, from the least to the greatest" (Heb. 8:11). Yes, variety is essential in order that God be complete, and completely expressed and identified.

Let us consider the Beauty that is God, specifically expressed as color. There are innumerable specific colors, but they are all God's expression of Its Beauty as color. Anyone who has ever experienced illumination knows that there is nothing dull or colorless about this experience. Indeed, there is color! Sometimes there are a great many colors in this glorious Light. This variation in color is a *living* expression. How could it be otherwise, when it is God, Life, expressed? In fact, it is all that God *is*, expressed.

Every specific expression of God, in all Its infinite variety, is absolutely necessary in order that God be complete and completely expressed. God does express Itself in an infinite variety of Aspects and Identities. No two Identities are exactly the same in all respects. Despite the fact that it is the same God, the same Consciousness, identified as each Identity, no two Identities or Aspects are exactly the same in all respects.

I might clarify this a little in this way. Anyone who makes pottery will tell you that he might make a dozen, a hundred, or even a thousand vases using exactly the same mold, using the same clay, colors, and designs, but there would not be two of them that would be identically the same. Sometimes the difference would be infinitesimal, but there would be some slight variation in each vase. In the same way, there are not two of us exactly alike. There are no two identical leaves, no two blades of grass, not even two snowflakes are exactly the same. Thus does God reveal Its Allness, Its infinite Joy and Beauty, in Its innumerable expressions of Itself.

Now we have a more clearly defined concept of the spiritual significance of that word *Identity*. And we can see that, although each Identity is specifically that distinct Identity, yet each distinct Identity is the same God, the same Life, Mind, Consciousness, expressing and identifying Itself.

# What Is the Body?

Our subject for this session is: what is the body?

However, before we begin to explore this important aspect of Truth, let us take up the questions that you have presented. Incidentally, these are wonderful questions. They show that you are clearly discerning the truth that God is revealing in this class.

The first question is, "Do you believe in eating meat?"

Actually, a whole book could be written on the spiritual significance of eating, drinking, and digesting food. I have seen wonderful things take place when this aspect of our existence was spiritually perceived. As to the eating of meat, this must be your own decision, and it has nothing to do with human will power. It will solve nothing to force yourself to stop eating meat through the exercise of the so-called human will.

However, there is one point that I wish to make clear. I abhor all butchering of any kind. Furthermore, I am convinced that this brutality will cease as our God Consciousness continues to expand in Self-revelation. But each specific Identity will perceive the truth pertaining to the butchering and eating of meat as that distinct Identity becomes more aware of his spiritual nature and the spiritual nature of all that is Life.

There is a fundamental fact underlying the mistaken practice of butchery. I cannot go into this subject right now, but I would refer you to the books of J. Allen Boone. In this wonderful presentation, you will discover that all Life, all Consciousness, is one Life, one Consciousness. In his book *Letters to Strongheart*, he explains his discovery of this important truth. He also reveals how you and I may also discover it. In his book *Kinship with All Life*, he brings out the necessity of perceiving all Life to be *one* Life. He offers proof of this truth through his own experience with Life in all forms. I firmly believe that every student of Truth should study the books of J. Allen Boone. In fact, I have had many letters telling me of the greater insight into the Ultimate through the study of his books.

I would say that it is better if we do not force ourselves to abstain from eating meat. We know that our taste in food changes as we expand spiritually. We do not try to change it; but we discover that as Consciousness expands, we are eating different foods and less of them. We also notice that we are less inclined to eat meat. In fact, we are not too much concerned about food.

Oh, I don't mean that we stop eating, or anything foolish. It is just that we are not so concerned with it, and it doesn't bother us to miss a few meals. You will remember that the Bible says it is "not that which goeth into the mouth" (Matt. 15:11) which is important, but rather it is the issues of the heart. This is true. If we do not make an issue of any of these surface activities, we find that any unnecessary surface appearances just drop away. We hardly notice it because it is so inconsequential.

Now, for our next question, "How do I make the evidence of Truth appear without humanly out-lining?"

Well, of course, we don't make the evidence appear. Oh, it appears, but never through human visualizing or outlining. It appears because you become aware that the perfect Nature is the only Nature of anything or anyone. I won't go further into this question right now, as the continuation of this session will reveal just how it is and why it is that the perfect evidence does appear.

The next question is, "Since all is Perfection, why the belief in imperfection? Where does it come from since there is only Perfection?

The belief of imperfection is a dream without a dreamer. It is the dream's dream. But to try to explain that nothing is "nothing" to anyone is like trying to explain what is in the middle of an O. The more you try to explain the what and the why of seeming imperfection the more you tend to make it appear that there is imperfection. It is "nothing." Of course, there *is* Something in the middle of the O, but that Something is not imperfect. There is Some-thing everywhere, and that Something is Perfection

Itself. God is All and God is Perfection. The belief of imperfection does not come from anywhere, and it isn't anywhere. If something seems to be imperfect, it is only a distortion of Perfection Itself. As you see more clearly, you are aware that Perfection always has been, is now, and ever will be. Thus, there is no imperfection to explain.

Now for the next question, "Do you think it better not to marry?"

You know, the Bible says that marriages are made in heaven. This may be true, but we know that weddings are performed on earth. That is, weddings have to do with the misidentity called man and frequently have very little resemblance to marriage.

However, I must emphasize this point: I *firmly* believe in marriage. But I do not believe that a wedding can make a marriage. We have too many weddings and too few marriages. Let there be no mistake about this—I do not believe that there should not be weddings. We appear to be operating in a world of social laws, and I do believe that we should conform to those laws. Let us render unto Caesar the things that are Caesar's. That is as it should be; otherwise the world comes down terribly hard. It is better all around that we have weddings. Nonetheless, I am convinced that a wedding does not constitute a marriage.

What is a marriage? A marriage can be compared to two halves of an apple that belong together. Suppose the apple were cut in half and you tried to fit a half of another apple to one of the severed halves. It wouldn't work so well, would it? Oh, if there weren't too much difference, you could do some altering here and there, and they would do all right as one apple. But really, they don't fit. They don't belong together because they do not make the one, whole, perfect apple that was already established. Frequently it is better to keep the two ill-assorted halves together and continue on after the wedding. This is particularly true if there are children.

Again, what is a marriage? A marriage is realized when you belong together and you know it. It is more than just being together. It is really being one. A marriage means that you are essential to each other's completeness. In fact, marriage is completeness realized and evidenced. This is marriage and it is beautiful. Yes, I firmly believe in marriage.

The difficulty is that we try to outline the companion. We don't get the little "I" out of the way and let God reveal our completeness. We don't wait until God reveals Itself *as* the one who is essential to our completeness. We attempt to leave God out of it, and thus we are seemingly leaving Mind (Intelligence) out of it. We are also misled into mistaking love for Love. We simply can't do anything of ourselves. It really is God who worketh in you (as you) both to will and to do of Its own good pleasure.

How do we avoid making these mistakes? First of all, by realizing that we are already complete—

that all that is essential to our happiness, joy, and completeness is already established in and as our Universe. Even though the one who is necessary to our completeness may not have appeared, that one will be made manifest in our experience if we first perceive our completeness.

There is much more that I could say on the subject, but we must get on with the next question.

The question is, "Since all that we experience is our own Consciousness, how can a silent treatment have any effect?"

In the first place, I rarely use the word *treatment*. To me, it has a connotation of something to treat, something wrong that is in need of help or treatment. Of course, a word is only what it means to you, and you will use the word *treatment* or any other word that feels right in your vocabulary. I like the word *revelation* instead of *treatment*. I know that all that can possibly take place is the revelation of the Perfection that has always existed and will always exist. In enlightened Consciousness, I simply see things as they are. But I do not treat or seek to change anything.

It really makes no difference whether the revelation is in silence or whether it presents itself as an audible voice. More often, it is silent. If it does come through as a voice, I am aware that it is not the voice of Marie. Silent or audible, it is God revealing Its own omnipotent Omnipresence to be all that exists as the one who has asked for help. But it is never the voice of a person. Actually, it cannot come audibly if we are entertaining any sense of person.

If I could give a treatment, it would have no effect. We are not in a world of cause and effect. We are past all that duality. *All is Perfection — constant, uninterrupted, and eternal.* There can be no cause and effect. If there could be cause and effect, there would have to be a time element. There is no time. All is *now*. If there could be cause and effect, there would have to be time between cause and effect. This in turn enters into all this false sense of delay in realizing Perfection. Later in this session, we will discuss further that which we once called treatment. Then this question will be more fully answered.

Our next question is, "Aren't most healings the result of expectation? In other words, a sort of self-hypnotism?"

If the expectation means that one is expecting something to change or be healed, then there could be some claim of self-hypnosis. But true expectancy is something else again. True expectancy is an opening of Consciousness to perceive the Perfection that already exists. In this way, expectancy is much the same experience as is questioning. We ask the question, knowing that the answer already exists or we would not be questioning. We expect the revelation of Perfection, knowing that Perfection already exists.

The next question is one that has been asked by many advanced students of this Truth, namely,

"Since there is only the *I*, there is no "you," is there?"

*You* is only another word for the *I*. Our only reason for the use of the word *you* is that we have to have some way of addressing each other. Unfortunately, we just have to use words. I could say "you" and "you" and "you." Yet I am fully aware that I am really saying *I, I, I.* So merely saying "you" does not separate the "I" from the *I*, when we know what we are saying.

Many teachers object to the word *man*. I rarely use the word, yet I do not make an issue of it because I know what I mean when I say "Man." Knowing this, I realize that it is just another little three-letter word for God. Let's not get too involved with words.

Sometimes, however, a certain word will have a meaning to me that makes it impossible for me to use that word. In this case, I avoid the use of that particular word, as it doesn't ring true for me. Then, too, the false word can seem to be confusing when speaking to another. Always, the important point is: what does the word mean to you? Then use it or not, as you like. Words are only so many letters strung together anyway. It is what you perceive spiritually, what you feel, that counts. "You" and "I" mean the same thing — the one Identity identified as innumerable Identities but *never separated or divided.* Consciousness cannot be divided or separated; neither can Mind or Life. *God is one whole Entirety, and God is not divided.*

Now for the next question, "What about pro-creation, the bringing of what seems to be matter into the world, only to teach it to work out of the seeming belief in matter?"

You know, really, there can be no such thing as procreation. That which we call man is not a creator. Even God is not a creator. I know that the Bible can be quoted as referring to God as a creator, but all of us know that there are many statements in that Bible that are just someone's opinion. This in no way detracts from the many beautiful truths that are presented in that beloved book. Nonetheless, *God is not a creator.* If God is eternal and complete right now, God has ever been complete. This means that all that is essential to His completeness right now is eternally essential to that completeness. Each Identity in existence right now is essential to the completeness that is God. So eternally, each Identity that is in existence right now is essential to His completeness. If God ever created one single Identity, there must have been a time when that Identity did not exist. If God brought an Identity into existence and that Identity died or passed out of existence, God could not be infinitely, eternally complete. There is no interruption in the eternal completeness which is God. And this means that each Identity in existence is as eternal as is God Itself. How, then, could God create an Identity? We will have more revealed on this subject during this session, but this is a good preparation for that which is to follow.

Now for our next question, "Do you feel that what we believe we see, hear, smell, or taste, rightly understood as Consciousness, is God expressing and identifying Itself?"

Indeed I do. When we go back of the appearance, when we see through that which is called matter, the genuine and only Existence is seen and understood. We perceive that everything that we have been misinterpreting as matter is here, all right, but it is not here as solid, dense matter. Every normal activity is taking place, but it is not taking place in or as matter.

Dear friends, it is in this "seeing" that omni-present Perfection is realized and manifested. This is a tremendous revelation; an entire book could be written on this one aspect of Truth. Yet it would not fulfill any purpose, as the words used in attempting to describe It could never express the beauty and glory of this Existence right here, when we really see It. No words of mine will ever enable you to see this Existence. It will be seen, all right, but It must reveal Itself from within your own Consciousness. No one can hurry this glorious experience, and no one can delay it. But this I can tell you: once Existence is seen and known as It really is, there can be no doubt as to Its genuineness.

This completes the question and answer period of this session.

Before taking up the subject of our work for this session, let us briefly recapitulate the three essential steps that are necessary to the realization of complete Perfection. You will remember that the first step was: *what is the Universe?* The second step was: *what is the Identity?* The third step is: *what is the Body?* Now, let us understand why these three steps are necessary.

To begin, virtually every one of us came up through some path of affirmations and denials, of giving treatments, visualizing, or something like that. Most of us have given treatments with the hope of realizing that which we called healing. However, as our Consciousness has expanded, we have inevitably arrived at the Absolute. Incidentally, the word *Absolute* is a much abused and misused word. We hear, on all sides, of this teacher or that author who is working in the "Absolute." Then we investigate, only to find dualism. But those of us who are really "seeing" that God really *is* All are not deceived. We know how far we have to go in order to claim we are seeing and being the *Absolute* Truth.

When, in illumined Consciousness, we become aware of the Absolute Ultimate, our joy is boundless. Our feeling is, "Ah, at last I am home. This is what I have been hoping to realize all the while." Then we begin to perceive that we can no longer give treatments, visualize, or in any way try to do something of ourselves.

It reminds one of the "little book" mentioned in Revelation that was sweet to the mouth but so bitter in the digestion. We know now that we have to go *all* the way in our seeing and in our *being* of this Ultimate Absolute that has been revealed. We can never return to the old way; yet we have not quite seen how Perfection is to be realized and manifested in this greater light. It is to help bridge this seeming transition that these three essential steps are being presented.

We now know that we cannot use a method. We cannot *use* Truth at all. We can't use a formula. There is nothing more dulling to inspiration than the attempt to use a method or formula. We sometimes feel as though we were floating around on a magic carpet but suddenly someone pulled the carpet out from under us. Then we say, "Well, what do I do then? There must be some way that will reveal the manifestation of this beautiful Truth I am seeing." Indeed, there is a way. And there is order in this way, too, just as there is order in the heavens. We don't do anything to bring this divine order into being, either. It simply *is*, and we realize it. In other words, we focus our attention upon the perfect order of all existence instead of treating for something to *come into* existence.

Right here I would like to clarify the use of the term *steps*. As stated before, we have to have words in order to present any truth. The word *steps* is not meant to indicate a method of separate steps. Actually, there are no steps at all in this sense. It is all the one Consciousness expanding in Its awareness of Its Allness, Its Eternality, Completeness, and changeless Perfection. But it is the One Consciousness identified as the specific Identity of each one of us. Of course, there is no such thing as the All God Consciousness expanding. But as this illusory sense of existence disappears, our Consciousness does expand in Its awareness of *being* this eternal One identified.

Again, let me state: there must be order in this "seeing." We just can't sit up here on a cloud with our feet dangling over. Let us take our lesson from the order that is manifested in the heavens. There is nothing haphazard about the movement of the stars and planets. Certainly there is activity, but it is orderly activity. This is an *active* Truth. This Consciousness is an *active* Consciousness. But all activity, all conscious activity, must have order because God is Omniaction Itself, and there is nothing out of order in God. God is Principle; God is Mind, Intelligence. All activity is intelligent Principle in action, so all activity is intelligent, orderly activity.

So it is that there must be order in the activity of our "seeing." This seeing is an active perception. We don't dawdle; we don't just drift along haphazardly on a rosy cloud. This does not mean that we go through a thinking or reasoning process — quite the contrary. But it does mean that we actively focus our entire attention upon the orderly, perfect Universe, the orderly perfect Identity, and the orderly perfect Body. We should be alert in this matter. When we are in illumination and the peace and joy are so beautiful and wonderful, there is the temptation to drift. If we are not alert, we may drift to sleep. This is not the Absolute way at all.

Does this mean that we do something of ourselves? No! No! How can we do something of ourselves when we know that of ourselves we are nothing, can do nothing, or be nothing separate from God? Yet we are aware of *being* this activity. We are active but never active of ourselves, apart from God. Furthermore, this activity is *purposeful* activity. Its purpose is not healing or perfecting anything. This activity is God fulfilling Its own purpose as our specific, purposeful activity. God, being the infinite, orderly Universe, acts and fulfills Its purpose in an orderly manner.

This does not mean giving a treatment or using a formula or a method. But any so-called Absolute teaching is incomplete that leaves us floating around haphazardly in the air. No matter how true this teaching may be, or how sincere, it is not complete.

True it is that the realization of the universal All as All is of the upmost importance. But this is not sufficient. In fact, it is but one aspect of the Absolute revelation. It doesn't help much to drift aimlessly around in the enjoyment of a detached sense of the Universe, if we seem to have to come down with a thud and then find the same old problems confronting us. But if we go all the way, if we perceive the perfect, eternal nature of the Universe, the Identity, and the Body, we are seeing completely, and this seeing is manifested as our Universe, as our affairs, and as our Bodies.

Certain it is that God is All. God is the only infinite Identity. But God does identify Itself specifically. God identifies Itself as distinct Identities. It is true that no Identity is a separate person or individual. Yet each Identity is distinguishable because each Identity is distinctly that Identity and no other. If this were not true, there would be no variety in God, thus no variety in the Universe, because God is the Universe.

So in our orderly seeing, it is essential to perceive the specific to be the All, identified *as that specific One* yet inseparable from the universal All which comprises all Identity. It is necessary to see this Truth completely. This means that it is essential to perceive that the All is the entirety of the specific Identity, but it is also necessary to perceive that the specific Identity is the All and nothing else.

God is specific in Its expression of Itself. If God is specific, we must also be specific. If God is specific in Its expression of Itself, we must be specific in *our* perception of Its expression of Itself.

For instance, suppose a telephone call comes in from New York. Someone cries, "Will you help me?" Now, your attention has been called to that specific Identity. But you know that all there is of that specific Identity is God identified. So you are immediately aware of all that God is. You are aware that God is the entire, eternal, changeless Universe; the perfect Life, Principle, Intelligence, Soul, Body, and Being that is the Universe. You actively contemplate this truth for a few moments. Then the specific Identity will appear in your Consciousness. You *are* aware of that specific Identity. But first of all, you are aware that all there is of that Identity is just what you know God to be and nothing else. This is being specific in your seeing.

There is nothing cold or methodical in this revelation—quite the contrary. A great flood of Love just pours throughout your entire being. I feel as though I am all the Love there is, in and as the Universe; and all the Love that is the Universe is all there is of me. It's such a warm and glorious experience. Sometimes there is even a warm flame color in this experience. But it is certainly Life alive as Love. You love the whole Universe because you are the Love that is the Universe.

Always remember: *we never include the specific Identity in our consciousness until after we have seen, felt, and experienced the infinite All—God, Good, Love— as the Universe.* I cannot stress the importance of this last point too much. First, feel and experience the

Allness that is God, then perceive this all-perfect One to be all that exists of the specific one who has called for help.

We do not give a treatment. We do not focus our attention upon the specific Identity. We don't send out a thought or project a treatment. Nothing like that goes on. It is just that suddenly the specific Identity is right here in our consciousness, and we are (without effort) perceiving God to be all there is of him.

Why is it so important that we first perceive God to be the entirety that comprises the Universe? Why is it necessary to perceive the nature of the Universe to be God before perceiving the nature of the specific Identity? *Because it is absolutely essential to perceive what God is as the All, the entirety of all existence, before we can perceive what God is as the existence of the specific Identity.*

There are other aspects of this too. For instance, if we first focus our attention upon the specific Identity, we are apt to be trying to give a treatment to a person. We are also going to be misled into believing that there is a person or an individual separate from God, someone in need of help. This means that we immediately try to do something.

And here is another aspect of this subject it is well to contemplate: in the realization that the Infinite All God, Good, comprises all that exists as the Universe, all personal sense is obliterated. There is no personal sense of responsibility, no personal sense of sympathy or anxiety, no personal sense of someone in pain, in need, or in trouble of any kind. If we are not clear on this, we are going to get caught by a false sense of responsibility, sympathy, and of trying to do something to help or to heal a person. No matter how fine our intentions are or how sincere we may be, it just won't work. The whole premise is wrong, and it cannot be made over into something that is right. We know too much now. We know that we cannot perfect that which is perfect eternally and without interruption.

Now you can see why it is necessary to perceive the Universe to be God as the very first step in the realization of complete Perfection. You can also see that this "seeing" is an orderly activity and that there is no dreamy drifting around on a cloud in this alert seeing. This is an orderly Universe. This is an orderly work. All activity is an orderly activity.

In our last session, we asked this question: "Why do we exist as an Identity?" We realized that each Identity in existence is essential to the completeness that is God.

In this session we are going to ask, "Why do we have a Body?" It is not surprising that we should question why we have a Body. So much of our difficulty seems to stem from the fact that we have a Body. I have asked this question many times when it seemed that my Body was so troublesome and so troubled. It dawned upon me one day that if I had a Body, there must be some purpose fulfilled in the inclusion of this Body in my consciousness. Then I asked, "What *is* the purpose of this Body?" The answer came at once, and it was very simple — namely, I have a Body because a Body is necessary to my completeness. I would not be complete without a Body. So long as I am conscious of a Body, this Body is included in my consciousness. Thus it is essential to my completeness as Consciousness.

Let us take this right back to the fact that God is all there is in existence as the Universe. God is complete. This Universe is complete. But would this Universe be complete without the bodies of the stars and planets? One might ask, "How do we know that there are stars and planets in the Universe? Is it merely because we see them?" How often we have looked right at those stars and planets and have been so preoccupied that we have not really seen them at all. Yet we know that they are there. How do we know that they exist? We know they exist because we are conscious of them. We are always aware that they exist. This leads us right up to the next revelation.

We know that there are the bodies of the stars and planets because we are aware of them. They are included in our awareness, our consciousness. We also know that we, as specific Identities, have Bodies because we are aware of them. They are included in our Consciousness. Remember, our Consciousness is our Universe. Just as the bodies of the stars and planets are necessary to the completeness which is the Universe so it is that our Bodies are necessary to our completeness. Yes, the specific Body is essential to the completeness of the specific Identity that you are. My specific Body is essential to the completeness of the specific Identity that I am. The Body is essential because it is essential that you be complete.

We should always remember that all that is true of God as the Universe is also true of God as each specific Identity.

Every truth in existence is a universal truth. In other words, every truth in existence is equally existent and equally true eternally and infinitely. There is no vacuum in Truth, and there is no area where the Truth is not in full and complete existence. There is not so much as a pinpoint in Infinity or a split second in Eternity that is not equally Truth-filled. Neither is there an interruption in the eternal Truth which is ever omnipresent.

Let us clarify this with a simple illustration. We know that twice two equals four, right here in this room and right now. We know that twice two equals four in the next room, in Japan, or anywhere else for that matter. The same truth is true on the moon, on Mars, or on Venus. It is the same truth being equally true throughout the Universe, and there is nowhere that this truth is not equally true. This is the proof of the truth being true. It is equally true throughout Eternity and Infinity. So the fact that the bodies of the stars and planets are essential to the completeness of the Universe is a universal truth.

Again, let me repeat: *your Consciousness is your Universe.* Just as the bodies of the stars and planets are essential to the completeness of the Universe so it is that your Body is essential to the completeness of your Universe, which, of course, is your Consciousness. In fact, everything that has existence is essential to the completeness of the one All-Consciousness which is God. In the same way, everything that has existence in your Universe is essential to the completeness of the specific Consciousness which is God identified as you. Furthermore, it is well to realize that there can be nothing in your Consciousness (which is your Universe) which is not entirely God, Good. If it isn't God, Good, it has no existence in or as your experience, your affairs, or as your Body.

Now, how do we know that we have a Body? Because we are actively conscious of the Body. It is in this same way that God is aware of the bodies of the stars and planets. God is actively conscious of the Body of each star and planet, but God is also aware of being the entire Essence, Activity, Mind, and Consciousness that comprises the Body of each star and planet in existence. Again, every truth in existence is a universal truth.

This section of this work should be studied and taken deeply into contemplation. There is tremendous power in the Truth that has just been revealed right here and now. Let It continue to reveal Itself from within your own Consciousness. Ponder this statement: "God is aware of being the Essence, Mind, and Consciousness that comprise the Body of each star and planet." This statement should bring the revelation of your Consciousness of your own Body. It may help you to realize that the Body which is essential to your completeness is comprised of your own Consciousness.

In fact, everything that is essential to your completeness is included in your Consciousness. It makes no difference what your need may seem to be, the essential Truth pertaining to that need is already established in and as your Consciousness. If it weren't so, you never would have been aware of that which seemed to be a need. Thus, there never really is a need; there is only the Supply announcing Itself. You are complete always and in all ways.

Do you see the universal Principle that is active in this particular Truth? It is this: God is complete. All that God *is*, It must express Itself *as*. God, being complete, must be Completeness. It thus must express Its Completeness as Completeness. The Completeness that is God cannot and does not identify Itself incompletely or as incompleteness, as your Identity or as my Identity.

This is Truth and it is a universal Truth. Completeness cannot express or identify Itself as incompleteness. This is equally true of the entire Universe, throughout eternity. There can be no incomplete expression of Completeness. God, as the Universe, is complete. This Completeness means that everything that is essential to the Allness, the Entirety, that is God is eternally established. Thus, the bodies of the stars and planets are an eternally established truth. If the Bodies of the planetary systems were not essential to the Completeness that is God, there would be no stars and planets. If the Body of each specific Identity were not necessary to the completeness of that Identity, there would be no such thing as a specific Identity being conscious of a Body. In fact, there would be no Bodies at all. There would be no such thing as a Body and no consciousness of a Body, if Body were not essential to the Completeness that is God. There would be no Substance in Form and no Consciousness in Form, if this were not an essential aspect of the Completeness that is God.

I know that we are now going very deep in this subject, but I also know that you are prepared for this further revelation.

Let your consciousness be "full open" as you contemplate this Truth, and you will soon be aware of the complete revelation of this truth of Body.

Now let us turn to our main question for this session: what is Body? Just what is the Substance, the Form, the Activity that is evidenced right here as the Body? Is it matter? No! No! No! *There is no matter. There is no body of matter.* God really *is* All. God really *is* the only Substance, the only Life, the only Soul, Being, and Body—and God is *not* matter.

God really *is* Spirit, but what is Spirit? How very vague most of the answers are when the questions pertain to the nature of Spirit. We are told that we have a spiritual Body. We can go farther than that. We have a Body that is comprised of Spirit. But what is Spirit? What is the spiritual significance of the word *Spirit*? Of course Spirit is God; but it doesn't help very much to know that God is Spirit unless we know what God is *as* Spirit. What is God as Spirit? God as Spirit is Consciousness.

Dear friends, this is exactly what we really mean when we say *Spirit*. We mean Consciousness. But Consciousness is awareness. You wouldn't be aware of anything if you were not conscious. Neither would you be conscious of anything if you were not aware that Spirit, Consciousness, Awareness, are identical.

Spirit, Consciousness, Awareness are all the same Essence, and that Essence is God. Indeed, we do have a spiritual Body. We have a Body that is composed of Spirit, Consciousness, Awareness — God. Just think of it: every time we have said that we had a spiritual Body, we were telling the truth. But we just didn't know how far we had to see in order to really understand the truth we were stating. Now we know. So the only Substance in Form is Consciousness. Consciousness is God. Thus, the only Substance in Form as the Body is God Consciousness being aware of what It is. This means God being aware of the eternal, changeless, Substance, Life,

117

and Being which It is. And this, dear friends, is the Substance, Life, and the Form of your Body.

God is Self-conscious. God is aware of *being* what It is. God is fully conscious of being all that God is. This means that God is fully aware of being Itself as all the Substance and as all the Form in existence. God is aware of being you. God is aware of being all there is of you. God is aware of being your Universe, your Identity, and your Body. But God is also aware of being Itself *as* your Universe, your Identity, and your Body, Your very awareness of being your Self is simply God being aware of being Itself as your awareness.

So you see, you do not have a consciousness of your Self other than God being conscious as your Consciousness. You do not have an awareness of your Body separate and apart from God being con scious of being your Body. I am asking you to see very far in this Truth now. The Substance in Form that is the Body is really God, conscious of being the eternal Perfection It is. God is the Substance, the Life, the Activity, and the Form that is your Body.

Does this startle you? If so, it is only because your eternal, perfect "Body of Light" has seemed to be obscured. An illusory picture of body seems to have been superimposed, making it appear that the body is dense, heavy, changing, temporal matter. Believe me, my friends, when I tell you that there is no such body In the Bible, it states that there is one Body and one Spirit, and this one is God. This is the

Body referred to in Luke 11:34. "Therefore when thine eye is single, thy whole body also is full of light." In order to see with the "single eye," you must be completely free of dualism. You must *see all the way*. This means that there is no created body of matter, no body that is born, changes, or that dies.

This is no new truth. There is no new truth. All truth is eternal. We are not the first ones to perceive this truth. Always, there have been those of enlightened Consciousness who have seen and known this Body of Light, and they have known that it was the only Body in existence. It can only *seem* to be startling because it seems to be a new truth to us. Every so-called "new truth" has seemed startling when it has first been presented.

That which seems to be a new truth always meets with opposition and with ridicule. If this were not true, those who have perceived this Body of Light would have been more open and insistent in their revelation of this Body. But has this ridicule, this opposition, stopped this Truth from going right on revealing Itself? No! Of course not. The so-called world will say that this is unreasonable. There is no such thing as a reasonable truth. If it has to be reasoned out in order to be seen, it isn't Truth. Consciousness does not reason; Consciousness knows. Consciousness is aware. Consciousness does not go through a thinking or a reasoning process in order to be aware. Paradoxically, inherent within each Identity (even those who ridicule) is an awareness of this glorious Body of Light.

As stated before, "The Body is God." The Body is conscious of being Its own Essence, Life, Activity in that specific Form. There is no use saying, "God is All" and continuing to accept the fallacy that the Body is something that is not God. Either God is All or God is not All. If God is All, the Body has to be God in Essence, Activity, and Form. There can be no Substance or Activity other than God, if God is All.

You are not dual. There can't be two of you. There is just one "you." There is just one Body identified as your Body. You are not both mortal and immortal. Your Body is not both matter and Spirit. There are not two kinds of substance in existence as your body. God is the *only* substance and God is One. There is one Something here as your body, and this Something is God, being fully aware of what It is. It is impossible that God could be the Substance, Activity, and Form that is your Body and be unconscious of *being* this Body. There is no unconscious Consciousness.

Indeed, there is Something right here where this matter body appears to be. But this Something is not solid, dense, heavy matter, blocked off in time and space. Right here and now there is the Body that is entirely comprised of Life, Consciousness, Mind, Intelligence, Principle, Love, Beauty. Yes, the Body is comprised of all that God is and of nothing else: "For I am the Lord, I change not" (Malachi. 3:6).

The Body is God being conscious of Itself. The Body is God, consciously being Its own Substance, Its own Life, Its own Activity, being Its own Form. God cannot be conscious of being what God is not. God can only be conscious of being what God *is*. God cannot express, identify, or evidence Itself as what God is not. God can only express, identify, or evidence Itself as what God is. Spirit cannot identify or evidence Itself as matter. Eternal Perfection cannot express or identify Itself as imperfection. Truth cannot identify or evidence Itself as a lie. Love cannot express or identify Itself unlovingly. Beauty cannot be ugly or distorted; It cannot express or identify Itself as misshapen or deformed. Contemplate these truths. I can promise that the revelation you will experience will be glorious indeed.

Now let us see just what God *is* as the Body. As stated before, God is equally expressed as all that God is. God's expression of Itself is equally expressed and present as each identification of Itself. If God is All, then All must be God. There is nothing in existence that is not God being Itself. We know that we include the Body in our Consciousness. So we know that there is something here that we call the Body. As God is All, the Body *has* to be just what God is, or there is no Body.

The Body is an actual fact. Therefore, the Body is an eternally established truth. Only that which is God is eternal. Only that which is God is the eternal, changeless Body. If we are ever going to see through this fallacy of the appearance of death, we are going to have to perceive the eternal nature of the Body and that the eternal nature of the Body is God Itself.

This means that we are to be aware that God is the only Substance, the only Life, the only Activity, the only Consciousness, the only Form existing as the Body. God does not partially express Itself as the Body. God expresses Itself as all that God *is*, as each specific Body.

Let us contemplate all that God is *as* the Body. God is eternal, conscious Perfection as the Body. God is the only Substance and God is eternal, changeless, indestructible, and imperishable. So God, identified as the Body, is eternal, changeless, indestructible, and imperishable. God is eternal, conscious Life. So God, identified as the Body, is eternally, consciously alive. God is infinite, eternal Beauty. God, identified as the Body, is infinitely, eternally beautiful.

Of course, God is infinitely more than these synonyms portray. There are no words that can possibly describe the Glory that God is. But these few synonyms can be considered as just a hint of what we perceive the Body to be when we know that God is the Body. We can contemplate any specific aspect of God—such as Love, Omniaction, Omnipotence, Truth—and realize that this is God identified *as* the Body. Not that God can be divided into aspects of Itself. God is the inseparable One. But this One is inseparably every aspect of Itself.

Now we can begin to get a glimpse of the actual fact: God is all that God *is* as each specific Body. And this, dear friends, is the "Body of Light" that we see when the "eye is single." That is, we perceive this eternal, beautiful, ever changeless Body of Light right where the Body of matter appears to be. But we can never perceive this eternal Body of Light so long as we continue in dualism. Remember, the eye (the *I*) must be single. "A double minded man is unstable in all his ways" (James 1:8).

In Isaiah 2:22, we read: "Cease ye from man whose breath is in his nostrils, for wherein is he to be accounted of?" This is a command to awaken and turn completely away from dualism. Here God states clearly that there is no accounting for this so-called man of matter with breath in his nostrils. Of course we cannot account for such a man or such a body. There is no mortal man and there is no body of matter. There is no human being. There is only God-Being. There is only God being *all* there is of that which we call man. This means that God is all there is of the Body of that which we have called man.

But it is not a body of matter, and it is not "man with breath in his nostrils." We are being commanded to stop misidentifying ourselves as a temporary, mutable man, subject to birth, change, age, sickness, and death.

Again in Isaiah 43:1, we find God saying, "I have called thee by thy name. Thou art mine." The spiritual significance of the word *name* is Identity. Here we find God saying:

> "*I* have identified My Self as thy Self. Thou art nothing of thyself. Thou art Mine. *I* have identified My Life as thy Life. *I* have identified My Consciousness as thy Consciousness. *I* have identified My Substance as thy Substance. *I* have identified My infinite Body as thy Body."

So you see, dear friends, it is impossible to claim our Identity in the name of Almighty God unless we know that God is our complete Identity, including all that exists as the Body.

There is another aspect of this Truth that it is vitally important for us to realize, namely, God is Self-conscious. God is aware of being all that It is. God is aware of being Itself as each specific Identity. God is aware of being just what God is, identified as the entire Substance, Life, Activity, and Form that is the Body. In other words, *God does not unconsciously identify Itself as the Body. On the contrary, God is completely aware of being all that God is as each specific Identity.*

Do you see what this means? It means that the Body is alive because it *is* Life. The Body is conscious because it *is* Consciousness. The Body is supremely intelligent because it *is* supreme Intelligence. The Body is perfect because it *is* Perfection. The Body is eternally, consciously alive because it is eternal, conscious Life. The Body is eternally perfect because it is eternal, conscious Perfection.

The activity (functions) of the body is eternally, consciously perfect because all activity is Intelligence in uninterrupted action. Thus, your Body is Its own consciousness of being eternal, changeless Perfection, and It is conscious of nothing else. "I am Alpha and Omega, the beginning and the ending, saith the Lord" (Rev. 1:8).

Where does this leave a body of matter? Where does this leave a body that was born, that can change and die? Where does this leave a body that is helpless before the delusions of sickness, age, deterioration, and death? Nowhere! There is no such body. There is no consciousness of a kind of body that sickens, gets out of order, develops foreign growths, that deteriorates, suffers, and dies.

In our textbook, *The Ultimate*, there is a reference to a boy who was hypnotized. Under hypnosis, he was convinced that an apple was fastened to the end of his nose. Was it really there? Did it actually have substance, form, and color? Was the boy really conscious of it? No! It is true that the nonexistent apple appeared to be very real at the moment. It appeared to have substance, form, and color. But the point to remember is this: that apple only appeared real to the illusory sense that was masquerading in the guise of the misidentity; the genuine and only Identity that was that boy never saw or felt an apple fastened to the end of his nose. So it is with us; our genuine and only Identity has no awareness of a dense, heavy, solid body of matter. When we are in illumination, when we are enlightened Consciousness, we know what our Body really is, and we have no awareness of a material body.

There is another important point to consider concerning the genuine and only Body. *It has never sinned.* There is no sinner, and there is no sinning body. Jesus knew this so well. In John 8:46, we find Jesus asking this question: "Which of you convinceth me of sin?" Jesus did not condemn or feel superior. He knew that the Mind, the Consciousness, and the Body were the same Substance, and that Substance was "of purer eyes than to behold evil" (Hab. 1:13).

Every one of us will come to the perception that there is neither a personal sinner nor a personal saint. There is only God, being God, as each specific one of us. If we persist in accepting the illusion of sin and a sinner, how are we going to help the one who comes to us bowed down with self-condemnation? If someone comes to us and says, "I'm just powerless against this evil; I'm just a miserable sinner; what am I going to do?" are we going to help this one by agreeing that he is a miserable sinner? No!

I have seen wonderful things take place when the so-called sinner realized that he had no human past in which he had sinned; that he had no weak body of matter that was constantly craving the things of the flesh. I have seen that which was called healing suddenly realized when the false sense of self-condemnation was eliminated and the glorious, pure Consciousness was revealed. There is no one who can tell me, and make me believe, that he is a sinner. I know better. I know that the truth of pure, perfect, conscious Being and Body has proved itself to be true. Only that which is true, the *actual* fact, can prove itself to be true, There is no sin, there is no sinner, and there is no sinful body.

Of course, we do not honor the illusion of evil by bowing down to its seeming temptations. We know that there is no personal evil, even as there is no personal good. We refuse to identify ourselves with it; thus, it no longer seems to associate itself with our Identity. It is not an aspect of our Consciousness, and it can have no existence in our Universe. Again, *our Consciousness is our Universe.* We maintain the same attitude toward the enticements of so-called evil that we evidence toward the temptation to be ill. Neither sin nor sickness has any existence. Thus, one can be no more genuine than is the other.

We do not condemn ourselves for the dream we seemed to experience last night. We know that we were never in the dream and that the illusory substance and activity of the dream were not our Substance or our Activity. We dismiss it for the nothingness it is. We do not fear it, we do not condemn it, and we do not try to overcome it. We just know that it is completely false and has nothing to do with us. This ends the matter. And this is a wonderful way to perceive the nothingness of the illusion of sin and a sinner.

Let us return to the question, "What is God as the Body?" We have discovered that God is eternal, conscious, perfect Life. Eternal Life can have no beginning and no ending. If It could, It would not be eternal Life. We have also learned that this conscious Life is the very Substance and Activity of the Body. Now we must ask ourselves, "Does eternal, conscious Life ever begin to be Life as the Body? Does eternal, conscious Life cease being Life as the Body?" The answer to both questions must be an emphatic no! There is no aspect of eternal Life that can begin or end. The Body is that specific aspect of eternal Life that is essential to our completeness. If the Body is necessary to our completeness right now, It is eternally necessary to our completeness. Thus, we eternally include the Body in our Consciousness, and we could never exist without the Body. This has nothing to do with a body of matter. There is no body of matter.

There is no such thing as a body of matter that is born or that sickens, ages, and dies. We cannot stress this point too much. There is no matter. God is All. How can there be a temporal body? There can't be. There isn't. There is no body that is born. There is no body that dies. We read in the Bible of those upon whom the second death hath no power. Who are those upon whom the second death hath no power? Those of us who know that we were never born.

A great spiritual Light once said, "The first death may well be that which we interpret as birth." Certain it is that the illusory world of matter is but an illusory distortion of the genuine and only Universe which is God. That which is called birth may very well be compared to the acceptance of the illusion called death. If we perceive clearly that we were never born (never experienced the first death) we can also see that there is no second death.

What is Life? Life is Activity. We would have no awareness of Life if there were no Activity. But in order that we perceive Activity, there must be something to be active. There is—and this Something is God, Mind, Soul, Spirit, Consciousness. All Activity is God in action. But remember, God is a purposeful God. God in action means that God is fulfilling Its purpose as Its Activity. All Activity is purposeful Activity. All Activity is God fulfilling Its purpose in being that Activity.

The activity that is going on in and as your Body this instant is God fulfilling Its purpose in being that Activity. Life is Activity. God's purpose in being Activity, in being Life, is to live—to be alive. God is eternal Life. God fulfills Its purpose as eternal Life by being eternally alive, eternally active as the activity of your Body.

God does fulfill Its purpose as eternal Life by being eternally alive as the Body of each specific Identity. Eternal Life is also eternal Mind, Consciousness, Spirit, and all that God is. This eternal

Life, Mind, Consciousness, Spirit, and all that God is, is the very Substance, Activity, and Form that is your Body this instant.

Life does not *begin* to be alive as the Life that comprises the Body. Consciousness does not *begin* to be conscious as the Consciousness that comprises the Body. Mind, Intelligence, does not *begin* to be intelligent as the Mind that comprises the Body. Principle, Self-government, does not *begin* to be Self-governing as the Self-government that comprises the Body. Conscious, intelligent, perfect, eternal Life does not *begin* to be conscious, intelligent, perfect, eternal Life as the very Substance, Form and Activity that comprise the Body. *That which has no beginning can have no ending.*

The Body is not a vehicle into which Life enters at birth and from which It departs at death. If Life entered the Body, It could also leave the Body. The Body is not a vehicle through which Life, Intelligence, Consciousness is active for a little while, only to suddenly depart. This is entirely a falsification about Life; but it has nothing to do with Life at all. Neither has it anything to do with the Body that is composed of Life and of all that God is.

If Life could enter the Body and depart from the Body, we would have Life, God, entering something that is other than Itself and departing from that something. If God could enter and depart from something that is not God, then God is not All. When we say, "God is All," let us go all the way in our realization of what we are saying. Let us realize that the only Substance, Life, Activity, Form in existence is wholly God and nothing else. If we cannot do this, it is better for us to stop saying, "God is All."

There are many who will tell you that the Body is Consciousness. This is true. And it is good as far as it goes. But it doesn't go far enough. When we say, "All," let us mean "All." When we say, "God is all Consciousness," let us be sure that we are including in that realization all the Life, Mind, Soul, Truth, Love, Principle, and really all that God is. God is inseparably One. Life, Consciousness, Mind, Soul, Spirit, Love cannot be divided. God, the All, cannot be divided into parts or into partials. *All* means *All*. There is no lesser or greater All.

Now when we say, "God," we can know that we have said all that God *is*. It doesn't do much good to say these truths unless we know and feel the indescribable depth and power of what we are saying. We feel and experience this glorious depth and power when we go all the way in our perception.

There is no Consciousness without Life. There is no Life without Consciousness. There is no unconscious Life and no inactive Consciousness. Life and Consciousness are One. There is no involuntary activity. All Activity is voluntary, for all Activity is Mind, Intelligence, in action. Thus, all Activity is intelligent Activity. But Mind, Intelligence, and Principle are One. Thus, there is no ungoverned,

131

unprincipled, non-intelligent activity. All Activity is intelligently Self-governing. Intelligence, Mind, always knows what It is doing. It never acts in a way that is detrimental or destructive to Its eternal existence.

This realization of God in action is extremely important when some so-called difficulty is functional. There can be no disordered function, no inharmonious activity, when we realize that the Activity which we call "functional" is intelligent Life, Consciousness, Principle in unopposed action. Always remember that there are no mistakes known to intelligent Principle.

It is true the Body does not act independently, and It is not separate and apart from the one, all-universal Activity, which is God in action. Yet because the activity of the Body is God in action, it is conscious, perfect, governed Activity. The Activity that is governing Itself as the universal Activity does not separate or divide Itself, because It functions as the Activity of each specific Body. We need to be very careful here that we don't fall into the trap of division and separation. The Activity of each specific Body in existence is the one inseparable Life in action, and It cannot be divided. Neither can it be parceled out to this form or that form.

There is nothing existing in this Universe that is not active. The leading physicists of today know this to be true. They have discovered that there is not so much as the most infinitesimal so-called particle that is not intensely active. They have proved this to their own satisfaction. Now, of course, this may seem to be departing from the high spiritual Consciousness we have been realizing, but there is a basic spiritual fact underlying these findings of the physicists. We simply reinterpret their so-called material discoveries into spiritual realities. At any rate, they will tell you that there is not so much as a grain of sand that is not constantly in intense action.

Not so long ago, I read an article by one of the leading physicists who inferred that there was Life, Activity, in outer space. Of course there is Activity in what he calls "outer space." God is all Activity, and there can be no vacuum in God. It is easy to perceive that the Activity in and as the air, sunshine, etc., is undivided and inseparable. But we are now prepared to see that this same undivided Activity is functioning as the activity of our bodies. If we can see this from the impersonal standpoint of the universal Activity, it releases us from the fears and beliefs attendant upon a false sense of personal bodily activity. Thus we can get the little "I" out of the way and perceive the undivided, impersonal God, Life in action, in and as our Bodies. I have seen wonderful proofs of this Truth, and you will also see this Truth prove Itself.

Suppose that Life, Activity, in the heavens were divided. Suppose that each star and planet had intelligence, life, and power of itself, independent of the All-Intelligence, Life, and Power. You know what the result would be. There would be chaos. If just one planet in our galaxy was capable of acting and decided to act of itself, our entire planetary system would be disrupted. It never occurs to us that we can change or help the activities of the stars and planets. These bodies are free from our attempted interference. If we were just as sure that God is capable of conducting Itself as the activity of our Bodies, we would have less difficulty.

Oh, my friends, can't you see that it all goes back to the fallacy of a little personal "I" believing that it is something of itself, can do something of itself, and can control itself, of itself? It is particularly important to realize the impersonal, perfect nature of God in action in the perception of the Life and Activity of our Bodies. If we attempt to divide this Life, we can be led into the fallacy that someone has more or better Life, Activity, than we have. We can also be misled into believing that someone has a longer span of Life activity than we are to realize.

Does this mean that the Body is not conscious of being Its own perfection? Not at all. On the contrary, each specific Body is Its own awareness of being eternally perfect as Substance and as Activity. But the important point to remember is this: the Body is not conscious of Itself as a consciousness that is independent or separate from God, the One All Consciousness. The conscious Life in form that is the Body is God Consciousness identified *as* the Body. It is conscious of being eternally perfect because it is comprised of the perfect, conscious Life which is God.

Yet God does not separate Itself from Itself as Its expression and manifestation. The manifestation in form, called the Body, is the one indivisible, conscious Life, specifically identified *as* each specific Body. "Yet in my flesh shall I see God" (Job 19:26). Yes, right where this spurious appearance of a body appears, we shall perceive the Body of Light, which is never born and never dies. This Body is comprised entirely of God and of nothing else.

How can we give a treatment to the Body of Light? How can we heal the eternal, perfect Essence and Life which is God? We can't. We don't. What can we do then? We can perceive our genuine and *only* Identity and claim It. We can perceive the genuine and *only* nature of the Body and claim it. We can see with the "eye" that is single and accept only the Body of Light that is perceived by this single *I*. We can refuse to accept this spurious claim of dualism, of twoness. But we must remember that this single *I* can only be realized by the complete obliteration of the so-called personal "I." Once this is accomplished, our Consciousness is "full open," and we really see and experience God.

Now, it must be clear that we cannot know the truth *about* the Body. We can only know that the Truth we are knowing *is* the Body Itself. Yes, the Body is the Truth. When Jesus said, "I am ... the truth" (John 14:6), he was not leaving his Body out of the statement. He knew that his Body was essential to the completeness of his Identity. He knew that if he was the Truth, his Body also had to be the Truth because his Body was comprised of the very conscious Life which comprised his entire Being. Thus it is with us. We, too, can say, "I am the Truth." We also know that our Body is comprised of the very Essence that comprises our entire Being. So we know that our Body is Its own Truth.

If we know the Truth, our Body *has* to know this same Truth, because our only Body is conscious Life identified *as* our Body. Do you see what this means? It means that the Body is completely aware of what It is. This awareness of Its perfection is constant and without interruption. Every aspect of the Body, every so-called cell of the Body (if we must name it) is conscious, perfect Life, fully aware of being eternal, changeless, and without interruption. The Body knows what It is because the Body is God, aware of being Itself, aware of being what It is.

Let there be no misunderstanding here. We are not speaking of a body of matter that can know anything, either good or bad. In fact, there is no body of matter because there is no matter. That which is called matter has no substance, no activity, and no form. Neither has it intelligence, consciousness, or life. In fact, it has nothing because it *is* nothing. But there is Something here instead of a body of matter, and we are discovering what that Something is. It is God and nothing else but God.

So often I am asked, "Is my Consciousness confined to the Body?"

Well, I don't think that we need to answer that question here. I am sure that all of us know that our Consciousness, our Life, is unconfined, illimitable, immeasurable. The Body is but one aspect of the Infinitude that is our Consciousness. We could call it a sort of "focal point." We could call it a "center," excepting that the word *center* implies a circumference, and there can be no circumference in Infinitude.

Any attempt to explain the Body by the use of so-called material examples must always be faulty. Yet it does help to clarify some specific point. So let us consider the following example. The light in the electric light globe (please disregard completely the light element or the flow or current through the wires—we are only concerned with the light itself) *seems* to be the focal point of the light. Yet it is not confined to the globe. The light that lights the entire room is the very same light that is focused in the globe. There is no division in this light. The globe does not separate the light in the globe from the light in the room. They are one and the same light. The essence and the activity of the light is the same essence and activity. This will give us a hint (though a faulty one) of the way in which the conscious Life that is the Body is also the conscious Life that comprises our entire Universe. There is a tremendous truth in this fact, but we must perceive it.

Never are we confined. Never are we limited or restricted. One of the most important words in my vocabulary is *freedom*. I insist upon being free; and I also insist upon leaving everyone else completely free. This is why I will not have an organization. This is why I will not function as a leader. This is why I say to each and every one of you, "You are free. Read anything you like; attend any lectures; read any publications; take any class you like. There is something of Truth in all of them." There is no one who can tell you what is your particular truth at the moment. You are the only one who can know that. Your own particular response will be to whatever should be revealed as your particular truth at the moment.

There is a fundamental truth in this necessity for freedom. It is this: only in complete freedom can we discover our God-Being. If we are bound by words, the writings, or the organization of others, we are not free to hear the voice of our own God-Being. This does not mean that we do not read spiritual writings. Neither do we stop attending inspiring lectures and classes. But it does mean that we do not bind ourselves to any leader or any one teacher. We do not restrict ourselves to the writings of just one author. We do not let organization limit and control us.

"Know ye not that ye are the temple of God?" (1 Cor. 3:16). Your Body is the temple of Life, the Consciousness which is God. And indeed, God is in His temple. Moreover God *is* His temple. God is the whole of His temple, which is your Body. Your Body is completely composed of what God is and of nothing else. I am sure that there are many of us who have seen this beautiful Body of Light when you have been in illumination. This is the Body that is imperishable and changeless. Once we have seen it, we can never doubt it, either.

While we are on the subject of Body, we must consider the word *Beauty*. We know that God is infinite Beauty. We know that this infinite Beauty must be manifested as every Identity which is God identified. Well, the Body is God identified. All that God is, is identified as each specific Identity. All that God is, is identified as the Body. God is the Beauty of Perfection, and God *as* the Beauty of Perfection is identified as the Body Itself. How can the Body be less than beautiful? It can't. It isn't. The Body is the Beauty that is God manifested as the Form and the Substance that is the Body.

This point is extremely important: in realizing the nature of your only Body, always know that all that God is, is identified as the Body. Thus, the Body is entirely comprised of Life, Truth, Love, Beauty, Perfection, Intelligence, Consciousness — in fact, *only* that which is God can constitute the Body. How, then, can the Body manifest anything that is foreign to God, such as an abnormal growth or an inharmonious condition of any kind? The Body can evidence only that which is essential to its completeness and its complete perfection.

Nothing is added to this Body of Light. Nothing is subtracted from It. Nothing is ever changed in this Body of changeless Truth. Nothing ever begins or ends as this eternal Body of Life; nothing ever becomes inactive in or as the Body of Intelligence. Nothing exists in or as this Body of eternal, conscious Perfection that can interfere with or obscure its Self-conscious Perfection. This glorious Body is Its own immunity to every false claim of inharmony of any kind. It is Its own immunity because It is conscious of being the eternal Perfection which It is. It can have no other awareness. In fact, there is no other awareness for It to have.

Let us again return to the Body of Light. Do you know that the Body is Its own Light? It is Its own enlightenment, Its own enlightened Consciousness. Let us make one more comparison with the light in the electric light globe. When we observe the light, we do not dwell on the globe. Oh, we know that it is there, but we are not specifically aware of the globe. Our concern is entirely with the light. The globe doesn't intrude itself; it makes no demands upon us; neither does it pester us. We do not dwell on the globe. We know what it is, and we don't bother any more about it.

This is the way it is with our Bodies when we really know what comprises them. We are aware that they are here. We know that there is Essence, outline, form, but we are not concerned with It. We don't focus our attention upon It. It doesn't intrude upon our Consciousness. We don't dwell on the Body. Once we know what comprises the Body, our only concern is in seeing and being the Light that comprises all there is of us, including the Body.

The Bible says, "The light of the body is the eye" (Matt. 6:22). The Light of the Body is the Light that is the Body. This Light is the one *I*. It is the one Identity identified as the Body. The Light that is the Body is the God Consciousness that knows Itself to be the Body. This enlightened Consciousness perceives Itself to be the Body of Light. Beloved one, this is your Consciousness, and your Body is this Consciousness manifested as Form.

Now the question arises, "But what about this seeming body of matter? What is it, and why does it appear?"

The answer is so simple. In fact, it is too simple. It needs elaboration. This seeming matter body is "nothing." But we have to go farther than that. So let us return to the simile of the dream. This so-called matter body is a dream body—but there is no dreamer. We are not dreamers. There are not two of us, one who dreams and another who never dreams. Nonetheless, this dream body is not the body of you or of anyone. It isn't a personal dream, and there is no person dreaming it. The dream is its own mass illusion. The dreamer and the dream are one and the same thing, and that is "nothing."

The impersonal dream illusion forms its own body. It forms it from its own dream stuff. The very substance of the dream body is the material that is the dream itself. The dream makes its own conditions, its own situations. They are all the impersonal dream, working away at its distortions of itself. But all the while, you are the same, changeless God being you. You are not asleep and you cannot dream. You can neither be the victim of a night dream, a day dream, or an illusory experience of any kind.

Is the supposed substance of the night dream body the Substance of the Body? No! It isn't even the substance of the supposed day body. There on the bed is this supposititious day dream body, while the night dream body has all sorts of experiences. It can seem to have substance, activity, and form. It can even seem to have sensation. Yet it has none of these, for it is nothing. It can seem to be aware of buildings, highways, cars, trees, bridges, and all sorts of things with which the day dream appears to be associated. Yet none of these things exist.

Now, I know the question you are asking. "Why is it that I *seem* to have the night dream? Why do I *seem* to have the day dream?"

Let us explore this subject briefly and see what is revealed. Have you noticed that you do not have a night dream about something that has no existence? For instance, there really are trees, houses, highways, etc., and these appear in the night dream. You do seem to have certain experiences in the day dream, and these experiences can appear in the night dream. However, more often than not, they are distorted pictures of that which seems to exist as the day dream.

Now, let us compare the day dream with that which really is fact, with that which really does exist. In actual fact, there *is* a Universe. This Universe includes the bodies of the stars and planets, as well as the Bodies of you and me. It also includes trees, flowers, cars, highways, and that which pertains to normal everyday living. But they are not material. *They are spiritual because they are composed of Spirit.* That which appears to be the day dream's dream also includes the appearance of that which really does exist. Yet there is no genuine substance or activity in the day dream.

The night dream seems to be a dream *about* the day dream. The day dream seems to be a dream *about* the actual fact of existence. The night dream is but the dream's distortions of the day dream. The day dream is but the dream's distortions of the actual facts of existence. The night dream never really touches the life, body, or experience of the day dreamer. The distortions of the day dream never touch the genuine and only Life, Body, and experience of the Identity which is God identified.

There is a tremendous light in the complete understanding of this simile. It enables us to see the whole fallacy of the belief that we are dreamers. It enables us to see that the dream and the dreamer are but the illusion's illusion about the genuine fact of existence. Seeing this, we are no longer concerned with either the dream or the dreamer. Let the dream go right on dreaming. It is nothing anyway; it has no significance in our God-Being and experience. We know the fact of existence. This is sufficient for us. God's Presence and Being is now known to be our *only* Life, Being, and Body.

We must not leave this subject, however, until one point is completely clear. There actually is no day dream and no night dream. There is no day dreamer and no night dreamer. This whole thing is in the realm of fantasy and has not one shred of truth or reality in it. God really is All. God does not dream, and God has no awareness of either a day or a night dream. You are just what God is as you; and you have no awareness of either a day or a night dream. But that which the fantasy of the day dream *seems to be about* really does exist. This existence is never material, human, or mortal. It is wholly and entirely God-Being. Now that we have discovered the fallacy of the whole illusion, we can dismiss it entirely.

Now let us see what takes place when someone calls for help or when we seem to be in need of help ourselves. This Ultimate Way is an orderly activity. We don't just float around on a cloud; neither do we dawdle. We cannot use this Truth. Truth is Its own Activity and proves Itself. There is no method and no formula in this Activity, but there is order. There is nothing that we can do, but there is something that we can realize. That something is the presence of the Power of God and the power of the Presence of God. We can and do realize that God is All, right here and now.

Of course, each one of you will discover your own way of going about this activity. But I would like to share with you the way that seems to bring the quickest realization of the Allness of God in my own experience, Perhaps this will help some of you to discover *your* way.

First of all, I find it essential to completely obliterate the little nothingness calling itself a person. "Of mine own self, I can do nothing, be nothing, know nothing, for of mine own self I am nothing." This prayer was given earlier in this book, but I must tell you that it is a prayer that is within my Consciousness many, many times each day and night.

When all false sense of doing something or being something of myself has melted away and I have claimed my God-Identity, I am "full open" for the revelation of that which is true and right, here and now. There is a feeling of expanding Consciousness. I never *try* to bring this about. When I am "full open," it just takes place. In this God-conscious activity, I *know* that God is the *only* One seeing or being anyone or anything. I also know that this experience is a God-experience; this activity is a God-activity. Presently I am aware that the *I* that I

145

am is the Universe, and the Universe is the *I* that I
am. I am not concerned with that which seems to be
a problem. I am just aware of God, my only Identity,
as being the only Life, the only Presence, the only
Consciousness, the only Power.

Often this is all that is necessary, and I have a
report that all is well. Again, I will have that inner
sense that nothing more is necessary. But if no
immediate report comes in and I don't have that
glorious feeling that all is complete, I know that
there is something more to be realized. Now I know
that I must be specific in my realization.

I am already aware of being impersonal, infinite,
tender Love. Now I simply include the one who has
called for help in the Love that I am. *But I do not
consider this one to be a person or an individual, separate
and apart from God.* Actually, I am acutely aware that
the One in my Consciousness is God being that
One. There is no separation between us, for my
Consciousness is that One, and that One is my Consciousness. It is a little difficult to explain in words.
It is just an inner feeling. But I can tell you that
Oneness in and as Love, Life, Consciousness is a
most glorious experience, and there is nothing
personal about it.

Now, suppose the illusion seems to be some
threat to life. My whole attention is focused upon the
fact that God is the only Life. God is eternal, changeless, perfect, Life, without beginning, interruption, or
vacuum. All there is of this One who has called, is

God *being* this One. Thus, all there is of this Life is God, being this specific Life.

There is no Life as the Life of this One that can possibly be in danger, be threatened, or stop being alive. There is only one Consciousness of Life and One conscious of being Life; there is only One aware of being alive. This One can only be conscious of being eternal, perfect, changeless Life Itself.

Of course, this is just a bare outline of what God reveals, but it may help you to discover the way that is right for you. There is nothing stereotyped in this realization. No one can know just how God is going to reveal Itself. Perhaps the very next occasion I have to realize eternal Life, God will reveal Itself in an entirely different aspect. It may have to do with Activity or functioning; it may have to do with Essence or Love. But I remain "full open," knowing that God is revealing whatever is necessary at the moment.

This same Truth remains true if the so-called treatment is self-treatment. I do not like the word *treatment*. It implies something to do and something in need of treating. The words *revelation* or *realization* better explain what takes place. God simply reveals the specific truth that does exist, instead of the illusion that *appeared* to exist.

You can see that there is no person and no sense of person in this activity. The fact that I have been specific does not mean that I have considered this One as a person or even as an individual apart from

God. It is all a matter of Consciousness and has nothing to do with a person or a human being. God sometimes reveals Its Truth in words. God will reveal Itself in whatever way seems necessary at the moment, sometimes audibly, sometimes inaudibly. But the words generally have this meaning:

> *I* am all there is of this One. *I* am the Lord; there is none else. There is none beside Me. There is no one existing but the *I* that *I* am.

It is a wonderful experience when God speaks and you know that *all is well.*

If the difficulty should be something pertaining to business affairs, I follow the same orderly procedure. God reveals the Principle, the Government, that It is, in and as all Activity. In business and in so-called human relationships and friendships, God reveals Itself as the Principle, the Love, the Intelligence, the Consciousness functioning in and as the stars and planets, in and as each Identity. So very often, God will reveal some truth in this way. This is why it is well to realize that every truth is a universal truth. God *is* the Universe, and God is all that functions in and *as* the Universe.

Should the seeming problem be a sick body, God will reveal what It is as the Body. You may find God revealing Itself as the bodies of the stars and planets. If the difficulty seems to be functional, God may reveal Its undeviating, unobstructed, irresistible Activity as the Activity of the bodies of the stars and planets. Of one thing you may be certain— God will reveal Itself in just the right way at the moment.

If there should be some seeming difficulty about supply, God will reveal Itself in some way as completeness. You will perceive that God is complete as each Identity. This completeness means that all that is essential to complete, free living is already present and manifested, in and as the unlimited, unrestricted nature of the Universe. God will reveal that It is complete, All. God will reveal that this completeness means complete awareness of abundance—of all that could possibly be essential to joyous, free living. Oh, there is so much more that God will reveal. But all of this is already inherent within your God Consciousness, and It will reveal Itself.

Dear ones, I can assure you of one thing: no matter what presents itself—no matter how hopeless or terrible the false picture may seem to be—you can always trust God to reveal Its truth instead of the fallacy that is tempting you to dishonor God by believing it to be true. You can trust God, you know. Furthermore, you *can* trust your God-Self.

> "I am with you alway" (Matt. 28:20). Yes, *I*, your God-Identity, am ever present as your only Identity. *I* will never leave you nor forsake you, for you can never leave or forsake your Self. *I*, God, am that Self, and there is none other.

# Summary of Sessions

In closing, let us briefly summarize the salient aspects of this Truth, as God has revealed It during this class. The first and fundamental fact is: *God is All; All is God.* We have perceived that God reveals Itself as the Universe, as the Identity, and as the Body. In this perception, God has revealed the answer to three basic questions:

What is the Universe? What is the Identity? What is the Body?

We have discovered that the Universe is God, the Identity is God, and the Body is God. There is nothing existing that is not God. The Universe, the Identity, and the Body are all one Essence, one Activity, one Being. The Universe, the Identity, and the Body are the same Life, Consciousness, Love, Beauty, Essence, and Activity.

God, comprising the one Universe, the one Identity, the one Body, does not separate or divide Itself by reason of Its distinct aspects of Itself as the Universe. God remains God as the manifestation of Itself as the specific Identity. God remains God as the manifestation of Itself as the Body. God is indivisible, inseparable, impartial as all Its manifestations of Its eternal and changeless Perfection.

Mind, Intelligence, Principle intelligently, purposefully functions as the orderly, uninterrupted Activity of the Universe, the Identity, and the Body. God is the Activity, but God is also *the Essence that is active.* All Activity is God in action. All functioning is God in action. Thus, all Activity is Perfection because all Activity is Perfection in action. All Activity is intelligent Activity because all Activity is Intelligence in action. All Activity is orderly because all Activity is omnipotent Principle in perfect, orderly action. All Activity is conscious Activity because all Activity is Consciousness in action.

Mind, Intelligence, Principle is intelligently governing Itself as the Identity and as the Body. God, being All, there is nothing that can oppose or obstruct the irresistible, irrepressible functioning of the omnipotent Omnipresence. This is Life Itself, and It is without beginning, without change, and without ending. It is also without interruption or vacuum.

Stated briefly: the Essence (Consciousness) that acts is the Activity (Life) Itself in action. Conscious Life comprises the Essence and the Activity that is the Universe, the Identity, and the Body. Conscious Life is fully aware of Itself as the specific Identity. The specific Identity is fully aware of Itself as conscious Life. Conscious Life is fully aware of itself as the specific Body. The specific Body is fully aware of itself as conscious Life.

The one Infinite All is essential to the completeness of the specific Identity, and the specific Identity is essential to the completeness of the one Infinite All. The one Infinite All is essential to the

151

completeness of the specific Body; the specific Body is essential to the completeness of the one Infinite All. Completeness is eternal; completeness is *eternally* complete. All that is essential to completeness is *eternally* essential to completeness. Thus, each specific Identity is eternally *that* Identity which is essential to eternal completeness. Each specific Body is eternally *that* Body which is essential to eternal completeness.

No Identity ever begins or ends as *that* specific Identity. No specific Body ever begins or ends as *that* specific Body. The Body of Light that is seen by the God-Identity is not subject to beginning, change, or ending. It can only be seen and It can only be known by the eye (the Identity) of pure Spirit.

The Body of Light is the Body that *is*. There is no other body. That which is called a mortal, a person, or a human being can never be aware of this Body of Light. When all spurious sense of being a person is completely obliterated, the Body of Light is seen, felt, and experienced. The complete surrender of all personal sense of self is realized when one knows that of himself he can do nothing, know nothing, be nothing—because of himself he is nothing.

Once this complete surrender is accomplished, one can claim his Identity in his right name, I Am. Then, and not until then, one can speak with authority and power because It is God Itself speaking as that One. When the Body of Light is seen, all is known to be Light. The Universe, the stars, the planets—and all existence—is seen as the glorious, indescribable Beauty of Perfection which It eternally is. There is no false sense of separation or division between the Universe, the Identity, and the Body.

Now it is seen and known that Life is always alive; Consciousness is always conscious; Love is always loving and lovely; Beauty is always beautiful; Perfection is always perfect. The seeing and the being (manifestation) are one and the same Essence and Activity.

Let us close with this quotation from the seventeenth chapter of John:

> And all mine are thine, and thine are mine; and I am glorified in them. That they may be one; as thou, Father art in me, and I in thee, that they also may be one in us.

Now we can joyously proclaim:

> I *am* Thou, and Thou *art* me. And the *I* that I am is the *only* Identity in existence. Thine is the kingdom and the power, oh God, and Thou art exalted as the All of all. As thy Light, I shall see Light; and the Light I see, that Light shall I know continuously, for I AM THAT I AM.

# About the Author

During early childhood, Marie S. Watts began questioning: "Why am I? What am I? Where is God? What is God?"

After experiencing her first illumination at seven years of age, her hunger for the answers to these questions became intensified. Although she became a concert pianist, her search for the answers continued, leading her to study all religions, including those of the East.

Finally, ill and unsatisfied, she gave up her profession of music, discarded all books of ancient and modern religions, kept only the Bible, and went into virtual seclusion from the world for some eight years. It was out of the revelations and illuminations she experienced during those years, revelations that were sometimes the very opposite of what she had hitherto believed, that her own healing was realized.

During all the previous years, she had been active in helping others. After 1957, she devoted herself exclusively to the continuance of this healing work and to lecturing and teaching. Revelations continually came to her and these have been set forth in this and every book.

To all seekers for Light, for Truth, for God, for an understanding of their own true Being, each of her books will serve as a revolutionary guide.

Made in the USA
Charleston, SC
11 September 2015